DUMBLE

Dumble
Tom Sackville

ZULEIKA

Published by Zuleika Books & Publishing
Kemp House, 152-160 City Road, London, EC1V 2NX

British Library Cataloguing-in-Publication Data

A catalogue record for this book is
available from the British Library.

ISBN: 978-1-7398212-0-3

Printed in the United Kingdom by CPI Books.

PROLOGUE

Those who knew my father Billy De La Warr, known affectionately as Dumble, generally admired, liked or even loved him. I write this in the hope that they, and others who did not know him, may be interested by an enquiry into how a man born into such promise eventually found himself battling with addiction, depression and despair, and came to end his own life in such brutal fashion.

On retiring from full-time work, I started collecting personal memories and views for a memoir about Dumble. While I realise he was not the usual stuff of biographies, in that he never made or aspired to make a great name for himself, I felt his many qualities deserved to be better remembered and recorded in print.

But he had an interesting and varied life. I have come to deeply regret that I hardly ever used our time together to ask him about his early years, his family's eccentricity, the war, his views on the class system, and what he felt were his own achievements and failures. What seems fascinating now was of less interest to a self-absorbed youth.

I originally intended this slim volume for private circulation, but emboldened by the encouragement of friends, I decided to risk wider publication.

Among those to whom I sent an early draft was a cousin and family friend, blessed with a sharp legal brain and a talent for getting to the point. Following various useful suggestions, he ended with, 'What a nice man your father was.'

My father could be forgiven for emerging into adulthood a little mixed up.

His family, the Sackvilles, were once described somewhat harshly by cousin Vita Sackville-West as 'a rotten lot and nearly all stark staring mad'. The influences coming down from his immediate forebears were unusual. His grandmother Muriel De La Warr was born a Brassey but showed no interest in the railways that were the source of her family fortune. She was an early supporter of theosophy, a bizarre cult which promoted an 'emanationist cosmology in which the universe is the outward reflection from the Absolute'. Whatever all that may mean…

More important, she was a considerable backer of the Labour Party and supported radical campaigns, women's suffrage, trade union rights and self-determination for India. She was on intimate terms with the leading socialists of the day, notably the pioneer and later leader of the Labour Party, George Lansbury. It was maybe these connections that lent weight to doubts as to the real identity of the father of her only son, Dumble's father, the charismatic 'Buck' De La Warr.

Whatever his paternity, young Buck clearly

inherited his mother's political enthusiasms. On leaving Eton in the latter stages of the Great War, he entered the Royal Navy Volunteer Reserve as a conscientious objector. This took courage, in standing up for his pacifist beliefs, and because the work involved great danger, including minesweeping.

His next move required equal resolve: with his mother's full encouragement no doubt, in 1920 Buck took his seat as the first peer to represent the Labour Party in the House of Lords, a position of splendid isolation he maintained for some years. This must have incurred the disapproval or even mockery on the part of more traditional hereditary peers, many of whom feared the old order was under serious threat from socialism, especially since the Bolshevik revolution in Russia in 1917.

I never heard my father discuss his feelings about his unusual relations. Nor did he boast of his long family history or appear to rely on it for self-esteem. But as he looked out of his window across the valley to the distant forest, he must have been conscious of the Sackville family's prominence in Sussex from soon after their arrival with the Conqueror.

The first to set foot on these shores, Herbrand Sackville, hailed from Sauqueville, today an unremarkable village near Dieppe. He held quite a lowly role as cup bearer, presumably meaning that he took one for the team in the event of an attempt to poison the boss. Whatever he did must have been useful, as he was rewarded sufficiently well to maintain a modest standard of life in Buckinghamshire. But the family soon recognised the possibilities of advancement through marriage. Herbrand's grandson Jordan was encouraged to marry a lady of Sussex some years his senior, Ela de Dene.

Ela had assets. Around 1200, the Sackvilles decided that her property, on a wooded Sussex hill just north of Ashdown Forest, would provide a seat befitting their growing status and aspirations. The family home, Buckhurst Park and what remains of the once substantial estate, is still in Sackville hands, in the person of my brother William.

The Sackvilles only made their mark on the public stage in the sixteenth century, starting with Richard, who served with distinction under various monarchs, and was rewarded with a knighthood. Becoming hugely rich, he gained the nickname Filsack, passing on his fortune to his children, along with an invaluable family connection. His grandmother was a Boleyn, making him a close cousin of Queen Elizabeth, and often addressed by her as 'beloved kinsman'. It is unlikely that his wealth and preferment at court did not derive at least in part from this. Monarchs of the day were not constrained by the attentions of the Public Accounts Committee or nosey journalists.

His son Thomas was a courtier, statesman and scholar. His accomplishments included co-authorship of the first English play in blank verse. Entitled *Gorboduc*, also known as *Ferrex and Porrex*, it was first performed for the court in 1561. It was said to have had in both style and content a strong influence on Shakespeare. His poetic talents won the admiration of his contemporaries: sadly much of his work, including much praised sonnets, have been lost.

Thomas entered Parliament aged twenty-three. Over the next forty years, he was a loyal courtier and favourite both of Queen Elizabeth and later King James, becoming Lord Treasurer and Chancellor of Oxford. Less pleasant tasks included visiting the cruelly imprisoned Mary, Queen of Scots at Fotheringhay to inform her of her impending execution. He must have done this with tact and sensitivity, for she rewarded him with gifts before she died, some of which are still in the chapel at Knole. During his time at the Treasury, his own wealth grew hugely, and the national debt also. He did however start the task of putting the royal finances on a proper footing. His fatal stroke in 1608 came during a blazing row with King James about royal profligacy.

His independently minded sister Anne married a Fiennes, Baron Dacre. This must have been a love match, as he looked unpromising. His father had been executed in 1541 for murdering a forester during a drunken deer hunt in Sussex. Following the loss of her own daughter, Anne took up charitable work and founded Emanuel Hospital to support poor children in Westminster. Little having been achieved by the time of Dacre's death in 1594, she set to work in earnest. Sadly, she died a year later, but the Queen took over and saved the project, of which she is now remembered as co-founder. Surviving from the foundation is the excellent Emanuel School, now in Wandsworth.

Anne's will contained a bequest of valuable jewellery and her 'land in Chelsea, Kensington and Brompton' to William Cecil of the dynasty which preceded and followed her brother as Lord Treasurer. Whether this was a sign of affection, a way of irritating a brother with whom she did not always get on, or an act of charity is unclear. But here was a family rich enough to show generosity to one of the other most prominent families in the country, a happy situation which has sadly not endured.

To suggest, as some have, a rivalry between the two families is a little flattering to the Sackvilles. In the sixteenth century, they had a considerable advantage. While the Cecils were making their way up the ladder through talent and skilful political manoeuvring, Richard and Thomas Sackville were royal cousins and insiders. Furthermore, we cannot overlook that for much of the next four centuries we were enjoying ourselves, while the Cecils bobbed in and out of public life. The late 1800s saw the emergence of Robert, known as the Great Lord Salisbury, serving three terms as Prime Minister and, during most of them, also as Foreign Secretary. The present incumbent of

Knole, Sevenoaks © De Luan/Alamy Stock Photo

Hatfield, another Robert, has won well-deserved grandee status, not least for his leadership and single-handed reform of the House of Lords.

Thomas went on adding to his fortune, building and aggrandising significant houses – Michelham Priory, Groombridge Place and, in London, Dorset House. The Queen had already given him Knole in Sevenoaks, which he transformed into one of the great stately homes of England.

Predictably, his fortune was then squandered by irresponsible descendants, with grandson Richard, remembered as a 'popinjay with pompoms the size of pineapples on his toes', leading the charge. This continued over many generations. While at their peak, the Sackville lands may have extended to more than 25,000 acres of Sussex and Kent, with more in Oxfordshire and elsewhere, my long-suffering brother scratches a living from a few thousand acres of unproductive Wealden Clay.

In the seventeenth century, the fun-loving Charles Sackville rendered valuable royal service but of a different kind. At the theatre, the winsome Nell Gwynne caught his eye, and through him attracted the attention of no less a personage than King Charles. She became not just a royal mistress but a highly influential one, bearing the monarch two sons, for the older of whom she procured a dukedom. This is the Sackville who, as recorded by Pepys, in 1663 relieved himself from a balcony in Covent Garden, appropriately that of the Cock Tavern, onto the mob below, necessitating the militia to be called out to quell the ensuing unrest. Within hours, the family church at Buckhurst was struck by lighting and burnt to the ground. The Almighty was evidently not amused either.

In the eighteenth century, the family got a leg-up from another monarch. Lionel Sackville had led a diplomatic mission to Hanover, and on the arrival of George I in 1713 was greatly favoured, carried the sceptre at the coronation, and showered with sinecures and titles. These included being created Duke of Dorset. In those days, if you made yourself pleasant at court, all sorts of good things could come your way. Lionel was not brilliant, but the great author and satirist Jonathan Swift was kind enough to call him 'one of the most agreeable and well-informed men, and best conversationalists'.

From that time on, as Dumble may have reflected as he surveyed the remains of the estate, the Sackvilles having acquired a great reputation in the sixteenth century, began to dissipate it in the eighteenth. The name came to be more connected with scandal and controversy than the dignity of high office.

Lionel's son, George Sackville, though a skilful politician and soldier, attracted huge opprobrium. This may have been unfair: he was later described by one authority on the period as 'the most traduced of all British Statesmen'. At Minden, he commanded the cavalry, part of an Anglo-Hanoverian force under the command of Field Marshal Duke Ferdinand of Brunswick. George had a low opinion of the Duke's generalship, and did not hesitate to say so. Things came to a head after the battle. Though the French had been routed, George had clearly hesitated in carrying out an order directing him to, in his view, recklessly advance his men through thick woods directly into enemy fire. Critics including the Duke put it about that he was guilty of cowardice.

The bitterness was undoubtedly exacerbated, although this is disputed by those who say George lacked interest in women, by his close friendship with the Duke's mistress. He nevertheless demanded a court martial, confident of clearing his name. Unsurprisingly, given who George was up against, the court did the precise opposite. He was declared unfit to serve in any military capacity, and publicly branded the Coward of Minden.

But he bounced back, taking advantage of the succession the next year of the new King George III. Meanwhile, as a favourite of his parents' great friend, the very wealthy but childless Lady Betty Germain, he inherited the magnificent Drayton House in Northamptonshire, having changed his name to Germain to please his patroness: the Sackville brand was at that moment hardly at its best.

By the late 1770s, he was sufficiently rehabilitated to become Secretary of State for the American Colonies, then in revolt against the Crown. Given that we were fighting an enemy defending their homes and freedom from an autocratic monarch, 3,000 miles away and effectively out of contact with London, it is hardly surprising the war was eventually lost. The calamitous British defeat at Saratoga was maliciously rumoured to be the result of vital orders, carelessly stuffed into the pocket of George's shooting jacket, failing to catch the ship in Plymouth.

In defeat, generals and political opponents need a scapegoat, and George provided a convenient one. His high-handed manners provoked bitter dislike among his peers. The sheer vitriol poured over him in speeches at the time of Minden, during the American War, and later over his entry to the House of Lords makes uncomfortable reading. But the warm support of those who had served and worked under him tells another story. Here was a man born to privilege but possessed of genuine real talent, not prepared to suffer fools. In those days, these fools included many in high office or rank unrelated to ability or merit but to their birth, and they did not enjoy being reminded of it.

The nineteenth century brought more trouble. The male line and the ducal title died out following a hunting accident. However, a daughter married into the West family, her descendants calling themselves Sackville-West, Earls De La Warr. The family then succumbed twice to bitter and very public schism. Knole was left to a younger son following the death of two older brothers, and the daughters of the family fought the inheritance in a long, expensive legal battle, eventually reverting to the name Sackville. However, Queen Victoria decided to intervene, favouring the winning side with a new peerage for her courtier Mortimer Sackville-West, as Baron Sackville. She may have felt she should dignify his occupation of Knole, a residence even more magnificent than any of her own.

Another controversy was the result of Mortimer's younger brother, the modest diplomat Lionel Sackville-West, falling passionately in love with a Spanish dancer known as Pepita, later famous as Vita's grandmother. Born Josefa Duran of gypsy heritage in 1830 in the slums of Málaga, Pepita had extraordinary beauty, grace and presence, becoming as well known for her waist-length hair and tiny feet as she was later for her magnificent jewels. Her ambitious mother Catalina, seeing her potential, tried to establish her as a serious dancer in Madrid but settled for European stardom, notably in Germany. It was there the romantic Lionel watched her perform and was smitten. Her name was at the time also romantically linked to several European grandees.

Lionel and Pepita could not marry, as she had made an early unfortunate marriage in Spain. Meanwhile, Lionel had on one occasion to be physically detained by the British Consul in Málaga to prevent him contracting a bigamous marriage to her and risking an even more damaging scandal. But he remained loyal. The couple set up house in Villa Pepa at the spa town of Arcachon near Bordeaux, calling themselves Count and Countess West. Lionel came and went according to the demands of his career, and fathered five children with her.

But it cannot have been a happy time. The 'Wests' were shunned by their bourgeois neighbours. Pepita could not even attend Mass in the local church, eventually having to build her own chapel in the garden overlooking the sea. The children found themselves friendless and in limbo, without being told the reason, most of them going on to have unhappy lives. Pepita tragically died in the course of her sixth pregnancy, leaving five children, all under the age of ten, effectively as orphans.

Victoria, the oldest, was in some ways the exception. Having survived seven years of what to modern ears sounds like systematic abuse by the Sisters of a local convent, she was rescued by her father and taken as his hostess to Washington, where he had been appointed Minister in the Embassy. This caused consternation at the Foreign Office in a staid Victorian age unused to such unorthodox arrangements. There was understandable concern at the reaction of the prim and proper matrons of Washington society. Once again, the Queen came to the rescue, letting it be known that she had no objection, and doubts miraculously disappeared on either side of the Atlantic.

No one need have worried. Victoria showed an aptitude remarkable in one so young for arranging balls and dinners, skilfully balancing the aspirations of the increasing numbers eager to attend. She had inherited her mother's magic. Washington society was won over by her beauty, sophistication and beguiling French accent. Men fell like flies, from the heirs to great fortunes to the President himself, luckily by then a widower. She received dozens of proposals of marriage. None of these seem to have tempted her. On her father's return to England, she met his heir, her cousin – also called Lionel – who against strong local competition convinced her to become his wife. She thus eventually became Lady Sackville and chatelaine of Knole, a role she carried out with style.

Victoria's extraordinary success may have further exacerbated her siblings' grievance and jealousy, denied the acceptance they so craved. It resulted in another famous court case. Her brother Henry, tiring of the farming life in Africa his father had provided, returned with plans to claim his inheritance of Knole and the Sackville title. It appears he went so far as to even deface the register of the Madrid church where Pepita had married. Lawyers and investigators were hired by Lionel and Victoria to disprove his claims, but the attendant scandal must have caused the family further unhappiness.

In the 1900s, Victoria's daughter Vita Sackville-West, granddaughter of Pepita, about whose life she elegantly wrote, became one of the most celebrated writers and intellectuals of the age. She played a central role in the Bloomsbury Group. Brought up at Knole, which thanks to her gender she was unable to inherit – a fact which influenced her later life – she and her husband, politician and diarist Harold Nicolson, settled at nearby Sissinghurst. Both openly gay, they were a great partnership, immortalised in son Nigel's *Portrait of a Marriage* and the subsequent diaries.

From Sissinghurst the multi-talented Vita collaborated with Mrs Jekyll to revolutionise English

gardening. Her legendary borders, with drifts of monochrome herbaceous perennials, replaced the more regimented approach inherited from the Victorians.

Meanwhile, Vita was herself no stranger to scandal, and I suspect not unhappy to be so. With charm and force of character, without conventional beauty, she broke up marriages through liaisons with the husband, the wife or both. Among her bridesmaids, Rosamund Grosvenor was a recent lover, and sister-in-law Gwen Nicolson (later St Aubyn) would become one.

If there was a loser, it was Harold's diplomatic ambition. He had participated in the Paris peace negotiations in 1919 and could have gone on to great things. But Vita's role as loyal wife survived only months into his later posting to Teheran. This did not put a stop to his career but must have put it under a cloud. In 1929, he resigned and embarked on a reluctant and unsatisfactory political career, at one time even supporting the fascist Mosley and later sitting as a Labour MP.

Vita's cousin Margaret Sackville, a respected writer, was first President of the Poetry Society. It has recently come to light that she carried on a passionate but discreet love affair with Ramsay MacDonald, the first man to become Prime Minister as a member of the Labour Party. This friendship was recorded in their many letters between 1913 and 1929. MacDonald, a widower, repeatedly proposed, but she declined and remained unmarried.

Dumble's aunts kept up the pace. I had the honour of knowing Avice Sackville as we spent many childhood holidays with her. 'Aunt Avie' dispensed huge warmth and a mischievous twinkle. But she had famously shocked the polite world in 1931 when she left her husband, Colonel Stewart Menzies, senior officer and later Chief of MI6, galloping off into the night and marrying the yet more dashing Captain Frank Spicer, one time Master of the Avon Vale and Joint Master of the Beaufort.

Her elder sister, Idina Sackville, went further. Feeling the strain of an open marriage and succumbing to hurt pride, she left her husband and their two small children at the marital home in Scotland and retreated to Kenya. There for over twenty years, she acquired and dispensed with five more husbands. Idina was part of the Happy Valley set. Admired for her sterling silver hypodermic, she and her friends lived a bohemian life of a kind rarely if ever seen at home. Among the multitude with whom she was joined in holy matrimony was Lord Erroll, eight years her junior. He attracted international notoriety for being found shot dead in his Buick at a crossroads on the Nairobi-Ngong Road.

The alleged perpetrator was fellow settler Sir Jock Delves Broughton, with whose wife Errol had been openly conducting an affair. Sir Jock was arrested and tried for murder. But with no eyewitnesses, the evidence was weak. Moreover, the foreman of the jury was his barber.

2

Despite his uncertain political beginning as a Labour peer, Dumble's father Buck De La Warr saw the light and more than recovered from his dalliance with socialism. He supported his aunt Margaret's friend Ramsay MacDonald, who by this time had fallen out with the Labour Party, and served in his administration in various ministerial positions from the Lords. He later joined the Conservatives and served under Baldwin. In 1938, as a young

Dumble seated in cap and dark jacket, in front of father
Buck De La Warr and PM Ramsay MacDonald

Lord Privy Seal, he supported in Cabinet the rebellion against Chamberlain's controversial Munich Agreement. Regrettably, he failed to follow First Lord of the Admiralty Duff Cooper in resigning.

When Winston formed his national government in 1940, the Labour Party, who regarded previous supporters of Ramsay MacDonald as traitors to their cause, kept Buck out of government. But following the 1951 election, Churchill appointed him Postmaster General. In this role, he introduced the international telex service, letter-sorting machines, the telephone numbering scheme and the transatlantic cable. He defended the introduction of commercial television against opposition in the House of Lords: I recall him telling me proudly of having ensured that advertisements would be shown randomly, instead of advertisers sponsoring programmes and influencing content. The way advertising is today allowed to disfigure commercial broadcasting would have appalled him.

Buck was generous of spirit and liked by his political colleagues, as he was by his tenants and staff in Sussex, and all who had dealings with him. In fact, he was adored by men and women alike, but I suspect the women had the edge.

He was spectacularly uncommercial: though not extravagant, he was the last of a long line of Sackvilles to get through life without having to submit to the inconvenience of a paying job. He followed a family tradition of living off his inheritance, selling off farms and properties once part of the estate. His agricultural career was bold and passionate but never profitable. Farming in that part of Sussex was always going to be a challenge. He and his Danish manager, Arnold Christiansen, were leading figures in the world of Channel Island cattle: maybe for this reason he continued producing high-fat milk from his herd of petite eyebrow-fluttering Jerseys, from whom he could not bring himself to part, long after most farmers had transferred allegiance to the high-yielding black-and-white beasts from across the North Sea.

My mother spoke ruefully of Buck's sale of the library at Buckhurst, symptomatic of how things had been managed. As the estate was handed over, he casually told a local book dealer to come and make an offer. He accepted the impressive-sounding sum of £50,000, which turned out to have been a fraction of the real value. At the ensuing auction sale, people came from far and wide to bid for manuscript battlefield reports by Civil War generals and other treasures.

Was this unbusinesslike approach a failure on Buck's part? It was hardly unusual among such families. Most of them persistently spent far more than they earned, were unprepared for vindictive politicians subjecting them to the fiscal torture of 'death duties'. Of the old families, the Grosvenors, still Dukes of Westminster, remain the richest. They were naturally prudent, with their business professionally managed. Of course not every family could be so prescient as to marry their son to a farmer's daughter against stiff competition, thus acquiring a snipe bog west of London later known as Belgravia and Mayfair. They also clung to freehold possession of anything they built, a vital contribution to their eventual fortune.

Buck's interest in farming was intense and worthy. As part of his deep desire to help our former colonies, especially in Africa, he further impoverished his family with an investment in then Southern Rhodesia, today Zimbabwe. He, with his friend 'Bobbity' Salisbury as partner, paid the then not insubstantial sum of £100,000 for Charter Estate, a vast cattle and tobacco ranch south of the capital Salisbury, now Harare. Buck loved

Charter, making ever longer annual visits, on some of which I was lucky enough to accompany him. Financially, it soon came to be seen as of doubtful future value, suitable only for my father's Younger Children's Trust. I am not complaining: at an early age, Dumble made me the largest shareholder, with a seat on the board representing our family interest. I learnt a lot. Later, Katie and I, and our children, visited annually and derived great enjoyment.

Charter was managed from the start by an Anglo-Argentine cattleman, David Worthington, a perfectionist. Everything about Charter was to the highest standard, from animal husbandry to staff welfare, its beautifully run school and church, wildlife conservation and the training of senior African stockmen into skilled riders in the *gaucho* tradition. There was no thought for profit, despite the polite protestations of the tolerant shareholders.

The succeeding years witnessed the tragic undoing of all this. A great nation was brought low by an opportunistic Soviet-backed incursion into Southern Africa under the guise of a liberation struggle. The violence ended with a timely cease-fire and Margaret Thatcher's inspired appointment as governor – the politician Christopher (later Lord) Soames, accompanied by his wife Mary, widely respected as Churchill's favourite daughter.

Katie and I were visiting Charter in the run-up to the ensuing election, the key outcome of the Lancaster House Agreement of 1979 between the various warring factions. Invited one evening to dine at Government House, as we sat round the Soames' dinner table, we found ourselves in a time warp, waited on by old retainers recalled to service after twenty-five years of the 'rebel' Smith regime. We witnessed British diplomats and politicians transported back to their nineteenth-century role, deciding the fate of nations over dinner. We were seeing British imperial soft power in action, probably for the last time.

Days later, we looked on as the votes were cast at the polling station on the farm, overseen by two grave uniformed Nottinghamshire PCs sent out to keep order. Nothing was said of the violent intimidation that, as we knew from our sources, had taken place in the staff compound overnight. We also knew that Salisbury was under siege, the suburbs increasingly under threat. Soames was highly unlikely to disqualify Mugabe: he had been tasked with finding an at least short-term solution to the crisis, and avoiding more bloodshed. In this he succeeded, albeit at great cost to the Zimbabwean people in the longer term.

It was characteristic of Buck to have made this commitment in a place so vulnerable and beset with risk. He could well have put some of the dwindling family assets in one of the clearly safer parts of the Commonwealth, in Western Canada or Queensland, yielding the huge returns they eventually did for some of his contemporaries.

Buck's interest in the welfare of former colonies was all-encompassing. He became first President of the Commonwealth Association, and a close friend of Robert Menzies, revered Prime Minister of Australia. If the West Indies were here for a Test, he would put on a charity match at the family ground at Buckhurst, inviting old friend Sir Learie Constantine, cricket legend and later first black member of the House of Lords; Garry Sobers, famous for being the first man to hit six sixes in a single over of first-class cricket; and local luminary Colin Cowdrey, adding magic to the home side.

I have dwelt on the preoccupations and behaviour of Dumble's forebears at some length as a factor in his eventual decline. By the time he inherited, Buckhurst was an exhausted estate. After years of imprudence, there was little cash or liquid assets. My father chose a career never likely to pay much, unlike friends who went to work in the City. He married a woman with refined but expensive tastes and considerable expectations. He nevertheless decided to keep up family tradition and move into a large house with an extensive staff, ensuring that his expenditure was bound to dangerously exceed his income.

3

What Dumble thought about his complicated background, and whether it weighed heavily on him,

Fishers Gate, Dumble's childhood home

to live up or live down to, is not clear. My main impression gained over the forty years I knew him was that he wanted a quiet life. If he could not be ordinary, he could at least do a normal job, without relying on past glories. In this he succeeded.

Later in life, following a distinguished career in industry, he claimed his real ambition had always been to own a TV shop in Tunbridge Wells. I can see what he meant, but given the chain retailers like Dixons already massing over the hill, it is lucky he never attempted it.

Curiously little is known about Dumble's early childhood. It was mainly spent at Fishers Gate, a comfortable, modest house next to the farm on the Buckhurst Estate. His mother, Diana, was a daughter of the Gerard Leigh family. They were originally from Bolton but later became extremely rich from property dealing in and around Liverpool.

*Dumble's mother Diana
De La Warr, née Leigh
© ANL/Shutterstock*

Moving south, as successful northern families often do, they bought the grand Luton Hoo Estate, where they lived and entertained in huge style.

But I remember Diana as warm, unpretentious and affectionate. One of my cousins called her 'gentle, kind and reassuring, in contrast to Grampy, who could get very cross'. She loved music and would sing as she worked in her rose garden behind the stables. The inscription in her memory in Withyham Church includes 'the hearth which was lost when she died'.

All I know reinforces my impression that Dumble was close to and emotionally reliant on his mother. He may have been affected by the problems she had with his father. Buck De La Warr was not just charming and liked by everyone who met him. He was also hugely attractive to women. According to various sources, he had many affairs, sadly for Diana including with some of her best friends. One of these resulted in the birth of a son, who later became the subject of scandal and hurtful public gossip.

All this must have caused pain to Diana, and probably Dumble and his sister Kitty. Diana found solace in strong friendships with women, including one in particular she knew through her involvement in the Bach Choir. I am guessing it gave Dumble a feeling for the sanctity of marriage, not so much for moral or religious reasons but from an ambition to give his own children a stable home, without the complications he had witnessed in his own childhood.

Among his early friends, we know Dumble counted Winnie the Pooh, Tigger, Eeyore, Piglet and Roo: apologies for such brazen name dropping. It so happened that A.A. Milne and his family, including Dumble's friend Christopher Robin, lived two miles away through the woods. It was claimed later that Christopher was bullied at school and later in the army for his cuddly connections, and blamed his father. Given the pleasure these small stuffed animals would give to millions of children around the globe, I hope that this was exaggerated.

I would like to think Dumble looked back on

his childhood as a happy part of his increasingly complicated life. He once said to me, looking at my then small children, 'You are so lucky: treasure these years – they will be a golden time in your life.' I thought about what he had said, and I remember wishing that time could stop, before the realities of school and adolescence reared their heads. Dumble was good to my children. He had a very kind heart.

I am pretty sure he had been a sensitive child. Psychoanalysis, far more unusual then than now, played a part in his early years. It seems Buck and Diana were keen followers of Freud: as a Cabinet Minister, Buck was able to help facilitate the great man and his circle's escape from Vienna to London in 1938, his daughter Anna having survived arrest and questioning by the Gestapo. Buck and Diana obviously assumed that regardless of evidence of clinical need, exploration of the workings of even very young minds produced some benefit.

Dumble was regularly psychoanalysed in early youth by Melanie Klein, who left Vienna a decade before Freud and became an important figure in the Freudian diaspora. We can have no idea as to whether this left Dumble better or worse equipped to deal with this wicked world. If we believed my mother's predictable opinions on the matter, considerably less. As it turned out, he was spared further Danubian psycho-dabbling by his removal to a boarding school at the alarmingly early age of seven. To some who observed his upbringing, this may have seemed a lucky escape.

These observers included Chips Channon, who wrote in his now famous diary after a visit to Fishers Gate in 1925:

> ... Buck and Diana are faddists who bring up their little brace of Hoppners in the most irritating way. Poor little chaps, I pray they may become desperate Tories. They are allowed no meat for fear it may make them sexual!

There is no way of knowing how he and his siblings reacted to their treatment, but I will pass on an anecdote from my cousin Belinda Giles, herself a doctor of counselling and psychotherapeutic psychology, which suggests it was pretty negative. Her late mother, Dumble's formidable sister Kitty, of whom more later, once expressed a sudden and treacherous admiration for Herr Hitler. This turned out to have nothing to do with political ideology. She was just grateful for petrol rationing having spared her the long drives to North London and back for her weekly psychoanalysis.

It is remarkable that even the more progressive wing of the aristocracy, as represented by Buck and Diana, seem to have found it quite natural to expose young children to the physical and emotional rigours of boarding school. Maybe even their democratic outlook did not preclude the need to have their boys brought up as little gentlemen. Or the demands of such parents' hectic social life meant the children came second.

Equally little survives about Dumble's time at prep school in Surrey. But his transfer after a year to another similar establishment nearby suggests to me that things had not gone well at the first. He nevertheless went on to Eton, an institution far from suitable for a child of a delicate and introspective temperament. I made the same mistake with my own children. We seem programmed to blindly follow the wrong path merely because it is familiar.

Looking back on my time at that famous school a generation later, I can see advantages: you get a great academic and life education, and leave with valuable scepticism about most other *isms*, with a resistance to self-important and dogmatic opinions, and equipped with a finely tuned 'bullshit antenna'.

But to be sure of surviving those five years, it helped if you excelled at something. This could be humour, sport, drama or scholarship – or you could be effortlessly rich or, in a phrase borrowed from zoology, become an alpha male.

It would be even more helpful if you were elected to 'Pop', the elite self-governing club of prefect-like seniors. This accorded you the privilege of striding around clad in white tie and tails like the great Astaire, but with the addition of a waistcoat worthy of a carnival king. Membership in those days allowed you to cane junior boys for real or supposed infractions of the school rules. Clearly open to abuse, and rapidly going out of fashion, this form of punishment lapsed in my time. Today it would lead to a charge of common assault – or worse.

Dumble was not remembered for any of these distinctions. His near silence about his time at Eton (one meets too many people unable to shut up about the wonders of the place) suggests it was not his finest hour. I imagine him as studious and hesitant, wondering why he had to spend so much of his life in this alarming patch of human jungle rather than the security of home. Hopefully he found kindred spirits who also stayed out of the fray.

He certainly came away with a healthy dislike of self-possessed extroverts playing up their class identities. I remember his characterising one of our Sussex neighbours as an Eton bully. Whether he had himself been a victim was not clear. But it may help to further explain why in later life he steadfastly avoided following the herd down the orthodox Guards/City route, in favour of more arcane activities.

I have come to understand that I am in many ways like him. Eton left him with a need to experience something quite different. In my case, I was packed off to Madrid for six months prior to going to university. The Pastor family with whom I had the good fortune to live as a paying guest were headed by the impoverished widow of an admiral. Deeply nationalist, Catholic Franquista, they were closely connected with all three branches of the military. But to me they were just wonderful people. Becoming part of their lives left me with a respect for other people's beliefs and provided a unique opportunity to rapidly learn a language.

The entire time I was with them, they did not speak a word of English to me, in contrast to the experience of contemporaries studying in Madrid at the time. This left me believing that I was a linguist, and I developed a burning ambition to learn languages. I went on to pursue this enthusiastically with varying success but in ways that greatly enriched my life.

Dumble had an even more life-changing few months at about the same age. Between leaving Eton and becoming old enough to join up, he was despatched to Bolton, Lancashire through the good offices of a family friend, boss of the then textile giant Tootal, Broadhurst and Lee. He lodged with a mill family in Farnworth, one of the more traditional areas of this solidly industrial town. By day he worked at Tootal Mill as an apprentice wet spinner, his real identity unknown to those with whom he lived and worked. He clearly made many friends. When I arrived in Bolton some forty years later as a parliamentary candidate, I more than once knocked on a door to be informed by a lady of a certain age, 'You look like your father. He was a lovely man – he used to open the door for us mill girls. No one else did.'

The experience of living on equal terms with

people from such a different background from his own taught him many things. It reinforced his fundamental belief, which many preach but fail to practise, that all men are created equal. All his life, Dumble was clearly concerned with how he treated people less privileged than himself. People of his own background he felt could look after themselves. I became increasingly aware of this side of him as I grew up, because I felt the same, or at least knew this was how I should feel.

Dumble was unconcerned with social pretensions. I recall one silly but furious row between my parents, resulting from their having arranged to give a prominent courtier a lift home from a party. The latter, with habitual modesty and good manners, suggested as we passed the Palace that he get out and walk the rest of the way. My father brought the car to a rather unnecessarily abrupt halt, despite it being clear to all that our passenger actually lived in another royal residence towards the other end of the Mall. In a trice, the flunky was out of the car and waving goodbye from a rain-soaked pavement. My mother was mortified: she set much store by her royal connections.

Dumble had a valuable ability to see past outward impressions, accents and education. Later on, unbeknownst to all of us, he used to interrupt his travels to the North of England, where his career with BET's cable TV provider Rediffusion often took him, to visit Bolton friends. Some people might call this inverted snobbery. I prefer to think that he had a genuine social conscience and respect for humanity.

I hope that he left Bolton, as I did years later, with the conviction that Lancastrians, especially from Bolton, can be relied on to reach the right conclusion on the big issues, far more consistently than their overthinking compatriots south of Watford.

4

Dumble then went straight into another momentous experience – five years of military service, including in two famous theatres of war, the Western Desert and Arnhem. In the former, he saw action at Tobruk and El Alamein. He never spoke about North Africa, and I deeply regret I never thought to ask him, but one can assume that these battles were intense and hellish.

But there must have been some moments of light relief. Ten years later, while supervising the restoration of Buckhurst, my mother descended a ladder to answer the door. From the scarf tied round her head, the visitor – a delivery man – clearly took her to be a member of staff. He had apparently served in the same unit in Egypt and was keen to tell the story of Dumble speeding through the desert night on a borrowed motorbike from Cairo to Alexandria for an assignation with a lady. As he proceeded to recount more details, such as why Lt Buckhurst's army nickname was derived from a simple change of the first letter of both syllables of his real name, my mother regrettably felt it appropriate to terminate the conversation.

Dumble never sought to join the Guards (by which I mean smart regiments generically) but obtained a commission with our local lads, the Royal Sussex, with whom he went to do battle with the Desert Fox as part of the Eighth Army. He must have made some friendships but none that seem to have lasted. The problem, if it was one, was of course the product of his own decisions. But it may mean that he had a different perhaps more difficult war than those who found themselves fighting alongside school friends and even relations.

For whatever reason, he clearly felt the need to carry on and do something even more challenging, and attempted to join the elite commando unit, predecessor of the SAS, the Long Range Desert Group or LRDG. Getting in was I suspect only achieved with the approval of Col David Stirling, their charismatic and unpredictable founder, and the LRDG was not short of applicants. Dumble was not successful. He immediately applied to transfer to the Airborne and was accepted into '3 Para'.

In 1943, a bombshell exploded in his life which may also have influenced his thinking. His dashing, extrovert younger brother Harry was declared missing in action. Harry was two years younger than Dumble and joined the RAF in October 1942. On 14 May 1943, he and New Zealander Flight Lieutenant W. J. Dooley were flying a shipping recce out of RAF Coltishall in P-51 Mustangs of Squadron 613, covering the Dutch coast from Bergen to Texel. Both were shot down. Dooley was rescued by a German flying boat vessel and spent the rest of the war as a POW. There was no sign of Harry – or his aircraft.

On the same day, Luftwaffe Feldwebel Max Winkler, flying a FW190 from fighter wing Jagdgeschwader 27 'Afrika' returned to base in Holland claiming to have brought down two Mustangs, one 20 km the other 45 km west of Bergen. This suggests the incidents happened too far apart from each other for Dooley to report what had happened to Harry. Meanwhile, the German account would not have been known until at least the end of hostilities.

Especially in war, there is no rhyme or reason to what happens to those left behind by tragedy. What to Winkler was just a cause for celebration and congratulation was for our family the start of years of pain and grief. My grandparents did not come to terms with Harry's death for a long time, if ever. My grandmother took an item of his clothing to a spiritualist quack, leaving with the assurance that he was in a German POW camp.

Given how much was known about his last flight, and the improbability of his captivity being unreported, it is hard to understand how she could have really believed this. But it is a testament to how the bereaved will clutch at straws, and how easily they can be exploited and their suffering extended by ruthless charlatans. It was not until 1948 that she finally agreed to order a memorial to Harry to be erected in the local church in Withyham.

Meanwhile, Dumble appears to have become convinced that it was he who should have died, not his brother. He had long believed that his parents cared more about Harry than they did about him or their sister Kitty, and it appears that others gained the same impression. Their Eton housemaster, the respected George Lyttleton, told Buck, speaking of Harry, 'Just remember you have another son.'

It may be an exaggeration to suggest that in trying to get into Special Forces, Dumble was intending to put himself in harm's way. But it may partially explain why he was happy to expose himself to combat perceived to be more dangerous and dramatic. If he was, he was for a long time frustrated. The Paras trained relentlessly and intensively for every sort of eventuality. But while other parts of the division were engaged in Italy and North Africa, Dumble's unit and others were held back, suffering many false dawns. A whole series of operations, some more hare-brained than others, were planned then cancelled at short notice.

The operation they were finally asked to undertake

was arguably the most irresponsible tactical blunder of the war. At least one senior commander is said to have called it a suicide mission before it even happened. Operation Market Garden, generally

Parachute Regiment 1944

referred to as Arnhem, was potentially a master stroke. The capture of key Rhine bridges would have allowed an early Allied thrust into Germany, shortening the war by several months. The arrival of the Allies in Berlin even a short time before the Russians could have saved millions of East Europeans from appalling mistreatment by invading forces followed by forty-five years of misery under Soviet tyranny.

But landing a small army by parachute and glider way behind enemy lines and close to crack Axis forces was always going to be highly dangerous. To succeed would have required not just surprise and precise execution but prompt reinforcement by armoured and infantry forces already in the area.

In the event, Market Garden did not benefit from either. Countless young lives, and the entire mission, were lost through poor planning and logistics. German units were all around, in far greater strength than Allied commanders knew or were admitting to have known. Many men were dropped miles from their target. Radio communications failed. The rapid advance across the ground necessary to reach the bridge at Arnhem before the Germans could reinforce, on which the whole plan depended, was not achieved. Out of the 10,000 British, Polish and other forces deployed, over 4,000 troops were killed, a similar number captured or wounded, with no more than 2,000 making it back to their units.

Like many people who have witnessed appalling

events at close quarters, Dumble did not talk about Arnhem. However, I realised over the years that for all his admiration for Brigadier 'Shan' Hackett and commanders on the ground, he nursed deep resentment against those in charge in London. There were considerable Allied forces, including a crack armoured brigade in position behind the landings. Dumble spent the rest of his life convinced these should have been sent to relieve the Paras. He believed they were held back because senior commanders hesitated to expose prestigious regiments to the danger of fighting their way up a narrow corridor defended by dangerous German units, especially at this late stage in the war.

He must have been also aware of the widely held assumption, spelt out in the film *A Bridge Too Far*, that Dutch resistance had informed London of the scale of German forces in or around Arnhem. This was backed up by aerial reconnaissance showing Panzers and heavy weaponry. But Monty and the others were determined to go ahead with their project. Not abandoning it was a huge risk, which eventually cost many Allied lives for no gain.

One evening, while we were having dinner in a restaurant, Dumble briefly opened up about Arnhem. My brother and I had asked him to tell us the worst things that happened to him in the war. He described running across a square under sniper fire, coming across a member of his platoon on the ground wounded and stopping to try to get him to a safe place. The man begged him to carry on and save himself. Seeing the young soldier's face rapidly turning blue and realising he was unlikely to live, Dumble understandably left him. Such dilemmas must happen to many in war. But I got the impression he wished he had followed his first instinct and that this experience had long haunted him.

I have sometimes connected this story with his decision some forty years later to publicly support the halting of the Falklands expeditionary force, then en route to the South Atlantic, to attempt a negotiated peace with Argentina. Such an idea of course ran directly counter to the clear resolve of the Prime Minister, who he admired; the entire Tory party, on whose benches he sat in the Lords; and the overwhelming weight of public opinion. He announced that in his opinion, these distant islands were 'not worth the loss of a single young life'. Caught up as I was in the prevailing war fever, and somewhat invested in the project as a past and future parliamentary candidate, I disagreed. But looking back, I now see that his was a courageous, lonely stance, and I wish I had later found an opportunity to congratulate him.

I have always heard that in the years following the end of the war, people were inclined to discuss who had 'had a good war'. Dumble had been in the thick of things but never got the recognition he deserved. He was mentioned in despatches following Arnhem and recommended for an MC. I suspected that if it had been awarded, he would have acquired that extra bit of quiet self-esteem that would have made the rest of his life a little easier.

5

The immediate post-war years were a trying, depressing time for most people in Britain. Those who returned from the war, though relieved to be alive, must have found everything a bit of an anti-climax. One of the challenges they faced was the need to get married and not to be left behind in the headlong rush to get fixed up.

I don't know when exactly they became an item, but Dumble and my mother Poppy first met in the 400 Club, one of the most fashionable of the Mayfair night spots conveniently doubling as air-raid shelters. Poppy had seen service as far back as the Battle of Britain, narrowly surviving bombs and strafing while serving tea and buns from a stall on Detling Aerodrome. She had worked as a volunteer nurse in Maidstone Hospital, including at the time of the disastrous Dieppe Raid, when she found herself putting dead soldiers and sailors under the beds and those still showing signs of life on top, all the while listing to Mountbatten on the radio taking credit for a great victory.

At her home in Kent, Guy Gibson, future VC

Poppy (in Red Cross apron) at Maidstone Hospital receiving wounded from Dunkirk 1940

and hero of the Dambusters raid, was billeted in the stables but did not seem to make much of an impression on her. She had far more time for Keith Joseph, commander of the ack-ack battery in the park, later to become a very cerebral politician, providing inspiration to the young Margaret Thatcher. Poppy thought nothing of dodging bombs, later Doodlebugs and V2s, ascending the Old Kent Road, heading for Berkeley Square to meet dashing young men in smart uniforms. These were heady days and nights, for many of the survivors perhaps some of the most vivid and memorable times of their lives. War was no picnic, but it was nothing like the years of degradation, arbitrary arrest and death camps endured by the citizens of occupied Europe.

What Dumble saw in Poppy was obvious. She was extremely pretty, with a mesmerising smile.

She had been much admired as a 'deb' in 1938, later boasting of having consistently relegated an ardent admirer, later to become a distinguished foreign secretary and peer, to the reserve slot on her dance card. What she saw in Dumble was also pretty clear. He was intelligent, not bad looking, capable of great charm and titled.

Poppy was a Devas of sturdy Huguenot stock but proud of her connection through her adored father to the Cawdor Campbells. Less to her taste was her mother's antecedence, the wealthy Campbell-Bannermans, who had moved south to a family home at Hunton, near Maidstone. In the 1860s, they had founded a wholesaling empire based in Glasgow, sometimes referred to as Britain's first cash and carry. Her uncle Sir Henry had a long and distinguished political career, becoming Prime Minister in 1905 for the three years up to his death. He was a well-liked figure and had a uniting influence on his party, credited in South Africa with healing the wounds of the Boer War. He has been called the last great Liberal Imperialist. But for Poppy, all that was only partial compensation for the unmistakable whiff of new money.

Meanwhile Dumble's noble but eccentric background and some of the attitudes he adopted must have worried her. She claimed to have been warned that the Sackvilles were 'odd'. But in those days the prospect of becoming a countess was still something to be reckoned with.

Whatever their superficial attractions, they had greatly differing outlooks on life, with little in common. My father was philosophical and questioning. His reading material was unadventurous, with heavy and repeated doses of Wodehouse, Waugh and Trollope. He was to my mind an intellectual. He had a remarkable recall of Latin and Greek verbs, and could be provoked into reciting the entire *Ballad of Reading Gaol* during Christmas lunch.

Meanwhile, he never aspired to a mastery of orthodox culture. My prep school headmaster, the dapper William Hampton 'Gervy' Gervis from St Aubyns in Rottingdean, was a keen supporter of nearby Glyndebourne and issued invitations to favoured parents. Dumble once caused some embarrassment by nodding off, snoring

Poppy recently married, Ulster 1947

45

increasingly loudly, and having to be repeatedly woken through all four acts of *Figaro*.

Dumble's likes and dislikes were various and unpredictable: in his quiet way he could certainly qualify as an eccentric. I remember his horror of root vegetables: these could only be grown if they were out of sight at the bottom of the kitchen garden, behind a tall hedge. He suffered from a phobia of farinaceous (containing flour, for those who escaped a classical education) puddings. He managed to pass this rare condition down to me, I presume genetically: I spent my school days bribing my schoolmates to eat my summer pudding.

He had other more expensive eccentricities. Dumble had a passion for caviar. It had however to be the best beluga. He suffered from fear of being stinted: if he could not be guaranteed a full two-ounce jar for his own consumption, he preferred to have none at all. I remember us all installed in a curtained booth behind a grocer's shop in St Moritz, where this rule was put into practice – and some.

He also once told me if he had to spend a night in a hotel with less than a five-star rating, he was at risk of sinking into clinical depression. I seem to have inherited something of this from him. During my twenty-year post-politics career as a trade association director, arranging conferences for top health CEOs from around the world, canny negotiation of group rates allowed me to follow Dumble's rule. All went well until the *Sydney*

Morning Herald were informed of the 100+ Australian delegation travelling to our event at the unfortunately named Four Seasons Ritz in Lisbon. Worse, someone had leaked an attendance list. The *Herald* ran a banner headline – 'Health Chiefs in 5 star Hotel and Luxury Cruise Beano' – naming the more prominent names. Luckily by then my retirement was planned.

A psychologist might conclude that this love of luxury and fear of mediocrity, which not surprisingly extended to choice of airline cabins regardless of what he could afford, contributed to Dumble's later problems. The mention of five-star hotels was the only time I heard him speak even in jest of depression. He may have been already fully aware of his vulnerability.

But given his early setbacks, what Dumble really needed was to excel. Early in their marriage, he and Poppy started going to St Moritz each winter, to ski and enjoy the scenery and the grandeur of the Suvretta House. Dumble took up the Cresta Run, an activity founded by a group of British officers in the 1880s involving a hair-raising descent of a steep icy course atop a tiny sled. Competition was fierce: the record holder remains Lord 'Rotters' Wrottesley, who in 2002 completed the descent in a fraction under fifty seconds. A Baron Raunchy is credited with the record slowest ride, with a time of 380 seconds.

Dumble was fearless, winning several awards

Junior Cresta Champion, St Moritz 1949

and at one point becoming junior champion. One of his many mishaps nearly cost me my existence: in early 1950 he 'came off Shuttlecock', meaning he flew into the air over the side of the largest corner of the run. As he landed, the razor-sharp runner of his sled grazed his thigh a few inches below the groin, days before the best estimate of my conception.

I have no doubt the handsome young lord's fearless prowess attracted the attention of some of the many glamorous ladies who always seemed, then as now, to be present in the racier ski resorts. I rather wish Dumble had been still at liberty.

He disliked many of the pursuits his new wife held most dear, such as racing. You would not find him at Ascot or the Derby, where the human landscape would not have appealed. He also showed no special interest in horses.

The local effort at chasing foxes, the Nevill family's Eridge Hunt, used at one time to hold a meet at Buckhurst, prior to pursuing the local foxes around our lake, usually in spring, so potentially destructive to my mother's beloved sea of golden daffodils. She was not a natural 'anti'. But for her, hunts should have names like the Beaufort or the Quorn, and she did not keep those feelings to herself. The arrangement did not anyway long outlast an incident in which following a meet at home, I showed off a precocious talent with a hunting horn from a top window, scattering what Vita once rudely called 'those red-coated fools' in the opposite direction from each other and their prey.

Dumble did, however, try his best to improve his shooting. He was a member of Gavin Astor's syndicate at nearby Hever and was happy to accept invitations each August to spend a few days at the rather magnificent Astor grouse moor Tillypronie in Aberdeenshire. Of course, he would never have heard the end of it indoors if he even thought of doing otherwise. Tillypronie was close to Balmoral, and for Poppy somewhere close to Nirvana, though it must also be said Gavin's wife Irene Astor was a genuine old and close friend.

But Dumble never really got the hang of it. His unreliable eye must have been the cause of deep frustration, and of course it was all very public. Over the years, I feared that trees were being felled to simply provide all the new-fangled Holland & Holland stocks prescribed by his instructors. Even eye patches were tried. I know how he must have felt, having been pretty hopeless myself. Shooting is a bit like one of my mother's admonitions on another important activity: it has to come naturally – you overthink it at your peril.

Dumble always proclaimed his admiration was reserved for tycoons and generals. An example was General and later Deputy CGS 'Shan' Hackett, under whom he had served at Arnhem. Hackett was an unusual soldier, blessed with great intellect and courage. Wounded before the final nocturnal escape from Arnhem, his life was saved by a brilliant German surgeon in the local Dutch hospital. Rescued by local resistance members, he convalesced for months in the back room of a heroic local family, despite the house being in full view of the enemy.

In 1942, Hackett married the widow of an Austrian army officer and was fluent in German and other languages. Following his final dramatic escape from Holland, he pursued a peacetime military career, rising to the very top of the army, later becoming Principal of King's College, London. He wrote a charming account of his adventures, and two novels about a fictional Third World War.

Dumble was also fascinated by people who built great corporate empires, like the legendary Sir Arnold Weinstock of GEC, especially those who had started life with few advantages. This belied a marked lack of patience with those who considered themselves special on account of birth. He especially admired innovators, thinkers and high achievers in business, science or foreign affairs. But he showed no apparent wish to be part of even the more cerebral end of the society of which he was by background a member. Some say it is easy to take such a high-minded stance if you are born already near the top of the pile and would accuse him of inverted snobbery. I prefer to see it as the product of his early influences and on account of being a genuine meritocrat.

Poppy was the polar opposite. She yearned for status and orthodoxy. She pursued movement in any vaguely upward direction. She felt most at home with people whose menfolk were despatched to the City by day, were seen at cocktail and dinner parties at night, and who departed on Friday afternoon for their own or other people's weekend homes. She was not so unusual in seeing this as the high point of what life had to offer, but hers was not a view shared by her husband (or her younger son).

She claimed to live by a number of golden rules. She made firm distinctions between those who knew how to behave – especially 'when to leave' – and who were therefore *sortable* in the French sense, and those who did not. Strictly Mitfordian in her approach to language, people who came up to town, or travelled on horseback in any direction, were not welcome. Her insistence that the Queen Mother should properly be described as Queen Elizabeth once led to a large bouquet finding itself friendless at the bottom of a gangplank at Southampton.

Poppy had a major weakness for royalty and those involved with it. Buckhurst weekends were awash with courtiers of all shapes and sizes, many of whose spouses were also 'in waiting' to one or other royal. But such friendships did not seem to lead to greater intimacy with her guests' employers. The only exception was the Queen Mother, who she met regularly staying at Spye, Gloucestershire,

home of Aunt Avice, for Cheltenham and Bad-
minton. Whether this was a disappointment to
her was not clear. It was certainly no bad thing
in one sense: in the presence of a royal personage,
her knees would turn to jelly and her discourse to
platitudinous gibberish. I do not think she would
have survived repeated exposure, either orthopae-
dically or psychologically.

I do not mean to characterise Poppy as a mere
snob. That would be to underestimate her many
qualities: her close friends spoke of her loyalty, courage and adherence to principle. In her
defence, she could not help being brought up and
influenced by a massively snobbish mother and
being sent to then fashionable Southover Manor in
Sussex. In the educational sense, this was only just
a school. It was more an Academy for the Avoid-
ance of Commonness. Some of its former pupils
seemed unaware that their class-obsessed attitudes
marked them out as the very epitome of common.

Nor would characterising her as a snob do justice to her role as one of life's rich tapestry of char-
acters. Whether she knew it or not, 'Lady Poppy'
– as her younger admirers came to call her – was
eccentric on a scale that even the great Wilde
could have struggled to dream up. Many of her
bons mots, especially about social and marital
matters, were the stuff of legend. She informed us
one day that 'second wives behave like mistresses'.
I am still wondering about that one but suspect

deep meaning. Sex, in her view, was something you just needed to get on with, without thinking too much: it could anyway not be expected to last more than three years. I fear that this advice was born of experience close to home. I will never forget her description of an attractive, charming young woman whose family were Sussex neighbours and approved of, and with whom her older son was stepping out, as 'quite unsuitable – she would go to pieces the moment he took a mistress'.

Her oddities attracted many admirers. One was a friend of mine from school, George Morpeth (now known as Carlisle), a colourful, besuited, snuff-sniffing peer, now sadly living in self-imposed exile in Estonia. He was once constantly to be found at Buckhurst weekends, often self-invited but always welcome, where his historical and genealogical erudition and wit were more than a match for the eclectic succession of fellow guests. From his Baltic retreat, he recently contributed a tribute to Poppy which concluded with the words: 'What a tragedy she did not live to see today's social distancing: something she had after all practised with huge flair and skill across Sussex, Kent and beyond, for over half a century.'

I have also always wondered why Dumble did not see warning lights, such as she claimed to have seen about him but evidently decided to ignore, during their engagement. He might have realised that such disparity in ambitions, attitudes and tastes could lead to a tricky cohabitation, at a time when divorce was a far from respectable option. Their marriage turned out to be a rocky ride, probably rockier than most. Being away at school for two thirds of the year, I must have missed a lot of the action, but during the holidays I saw enough. There were bitter rows. Most involved verbal rather than physical violence. Luckily, few progressed as far as the occasion when kicking a football behind the house, I heard a commotion from the direction of the butler's pantry. I peered through the window and saw to my amazement my parents on the floor locked in what appeared to be a wrestling match.

I know now that my proper reaction would have been to summon help, but my instinct told me this would have merely given the oxygen of publicity to matters that should remain inside the immediate family circle. I did nothing and slunk off, having decided the need for discretion probably out-weighed the risk of a fatality. I anyway observed that in the matter of unarmed combat, despite one party having had the benefit of intensive wartime commando training, they seemed evenly matched. I wondered later, having observed some of the more bizarre activities of our ferrets, Jimmy and Freddie, who lived in a run outside the said pantry, if I could have misinterpreted the nature of the incident. In any case, in the best British tradition, nothing was said, and life went on – but I was left wondering if it had given my mother some moral high ground.

On another occasion, my brother was coming up the drive from the pub and was beckoned to stop by Dumble, who informed him in no uncertain terms that he had had enough and was leaving. He would contact his lawyers from the first available telephone box. What happened next I know not, but an hour later everything appeared calm for family lunch, and normal service had resumed. Someone may have reminded him of the reality – that there was no cash available for a divorce settlement. This could only happen through the sale of the house and estate, and that after nearly a thousand years of possession, this would be a pity.

They remained married for forty-two years. It would have been longer but for Dumble's untimely end. I like to think that he saw some benefit from being married to a woman so different from himself, who possessed such certainty and conviction. He may have secretly admired the fact that for Poppy, where financial and social advantage were concerned, you took no prisoners. And there were times when he may have needed her support and her courage under fire. I also recognise that both of them felt they had a duty to stay together for the sake of us children, for which I am grateful to both of them.

I was struck at quite a young age by the story, told to us by Poppy herself, in a café in the Champs-Élysées, I recall, of the woman from Birmingham. This may sound like the prelude to a limerick but was actually something of a cautionary tale.

On one of his tiring perambulations around the regions of England for his employer, perhaps in pursuit of some evening relaxation, Dumble befriended a woman in a casino. One thing led to another, and over the ensuing weeks and months, payments were demanded and made. Poor Dumble was soon in a hell of a mess, bedbound and suffering from another nervous breakdown. Then things started to happen. The chain of command was as follows: the psychiatrist to whom the details were first confided told the GP, who told the family lawyers, who told Poppy, at which point a senior policeman was consulted.

Luckily for Dumble, in those days lawyers were less in thrall to attorney-client privilege, as were doctors to patient confidentiality. The story was able to rapidly reach the ears of those needing to know but not those who did not. The Police and Criminal Act was a good twenty years away. In the privacy of some dingy basement cell, in the absence of tape recorders, cameras or other inhibiting safeguards, the loyal constabulary doubtless took the opportunity to remind the wretched blackmailer of her rights – or lack of them. She was probably informed of the inadvisability of further contact with this or any other lord a leaping she might encounter. No further demands were received and the crisis averted. Again, Poppy came away in possession of a further tract of moral high ground.

Earlier on in the marriage, Dumble had seriously

tested his new bride's loyalty by setting up shop just north of the Irish border. Whatever Poppy must have hoped for from married life, this was very different. Instead of a comfortable, fashionable life waving goodbye each morning to a City gent, she found herself for the next year housed in the upper floor of a pub in Newry. Dumble was working at the nearby textile firm Moygashel, learning the intricacies of the weaving business. Although somewhat alleviated by weekends at various local statelies, she always maintained that this interlude had led to the breakdown of her health, both physically and (by implication, as these things were rarely admitted) mentally.

Poppy developed a bad case of pneumonia. She also acquired a lifelong suspicion of all things Roman Catholic, later recounting memories of how those who had won money at the races had to swear the rest of the village to secrecy, before the priest heard of it and came knocking. In any case, Dumble's life at the coalface of the textile business came to an accelerated end, and they returned to London.

This allowed Poppy to live a more conventional life. At one point, they enjoyed the luxury of access to a suite at very favourable rates in the Ritz, which happened to be just across Piccadilly from Dumble's new office. But they soon acquired a five-storey house in Wilton Street, remaining there until 1954, when they moved to Sussex. I suspect this was a relatively happy time. It was an elegant house, in one of those now much sought after streets between Belgrave Square and the back wall of the Palace – the sort of area to which the native British can now no longer even aspire.

The neighbours included eminent people. If we children grazed our knees or developed a cough, Dr Sheldon, who lived across the street, was summoned. Sir Wilfrid Sheldon, as he was later known, was not just any doctor: he was a giant in the emerging field of paediatric medicine and served as the Physician-Paediatrician to the royal household, constitutionally a rather key job. Poppy had a strong belief in the omniscience of royal doctors.

Next door lived General (later Field Marshal) Sir Gerald Templer. Vastly respected as a soldier in two world wars, he came to wider public notice as a member of the Control Commission, the body which governed occupied Germany – he famously fired the Mayor of Cologne, later to become German chancellor, Konrad Adenauer for 'laziness and inefficiency'. Templer was notably short-tempered. At a dinner in Jordan, he was remembered for shouting at the King and repeatedly banging the table, having been infuriated by some attitude struck by the Hashemite ruler.

Less well known was an incident in Wilton Street, in which the general, with Dumble in support, pursued a suspected burglar, knocked him off his stolen bicycle and 'nearly killed him' while carrying out a citizen's arrest. In those days, between a general and a half-dead burglar, your average bobby knew which side he was on.

I suspect the intention from the beginning had always been to live at Buckhurst and make the necessary massive investment (which they could not remotely afford) to bring this increasingly derelict pile back to its former glory. This decision was, according to my father, Poppy's but according to her entirely his. Either way, it was a challenge. The work involved not just restoring and decorating a large early Victorian house while demolishing various later additions. Some of these were the work of the esteemed Augustus Pugin, but that was not enough for them to be deemed worth preserving.

Buckhurst, family home from 1954

Whether Dumble was bullied into moving to Buckhurst or not, he could not have been entirely displeased with the result. He found himself in possession of an imposing, architecturally interesting and now extremely comfortable house. It boasted an important sunken garden and hanging terraces designed by the great Edwin Lutyens. From the head of a long, highly polished dining table, Dumble looked past his family and guests across parkland to a series of lakes and beyond to Ashdown Forest, master of all he surveyed.

Poppy had in fact created a home worthy of inviting anyone, however grand, for weekends and, in particular, Sunday lunches. Dumble may have found some of the guests intellectually unchallenging despite their being civilised, charming people. But this would have been more than compensated by the inclusion of many who were much to his taste – senior diplomats, visiting members of President Reagan's 'kitchen cabinet' they had met in Washington; Edward's Heath's elderly parents, who happened to live not far away in Kent; and Dennis and Margaret Thatcher, who in those early days did also. Among many regular guests were Douglas and Mary Lee Fairbanks and their family, and the Spanish Ambassador Pepe Santa Cruz and his splendid wife Casilda.

The Fairbanks were attractive and gregarious, and had always spent a lot of time in London where they were in much demand. Douglas had far more to him than many of his profession. I remember his witticism in the visitors' book following a weekend during which we had all been to lunch with the Astors at Hever: 'Tom had flown in overnight from New York and drove to lunch from the airport – *per ardua ad Astor.*'

The Macmillan clan were conveniently based at Birch Grove, just the other side of Ashdown Forest. For temporary respite from SuperMac's (Harold's) many demands, it suited daughter-in-law Katie to send the great man over to us for Sunday lunch, where he was not only extremely welcome but always found an appreciative audience. It greatly suited my parents to provide for the entertainment of their guests a legendary former Prime Minister, revered by many Americans as not only a statesman of the old school but an intimate of the late Jack Kennedy. Moving smoothly into raconteur mode, the great man had the gift of bringing recent history to life, reminiscing brilliantly about the war, Churchill, Suez and purveying high-value gossip from around the post-war world.

There were also many younger guests whose company Dumble enjoyed. He was most comfortable in the company of women, naturally skilled at extracting confidences which they might have preferred to have kept secret. But he was never a gossip. He had a soft spot for the irresistible Emma Chetwode, who stayed with us from time to time: they would sit next to each other at dinner, purring away. Many years later, he used to stay with her on his travels, when as consort of the Taipan of Jardines, Simon Keswick, she ruled over Hong Kong. He also got on famously with my future wife, the widely admired beauty Katie Windsor-Lewis. He was fond of my Oxford contemporary Gully Wells, sharp-witted stepdaughter of the eminent philosopher Professor Freddie Ayer. Of my childhood friend Michael Waterhouse he used to say, 'I like having Mike around – he always cheers me up.'

6

Dumble needed cheering up. Since quite early on he had suffered bouts of depression, of which I can clearly remember two, during which we were just told he had retired to bed. I realised later that he was being treated by a psychiatrist and had developed a dependence on, by today's standards, pretty brutal psychotherapeutic drugs. I have always wondered whether his early exposure to psychoanalysis was a factor, and whether his choices of military and business career, in a heroic and probably often lonely struggle to do things his way, actually made things worse.

A solution would have been to move on from his worthy but unglamorous professional existence, with its debilitating daily commutes to London, to something more vocational and intellectually

ELECTION ADDRESS
N.E. BETHNAL GREEN

from

BILL BUCKHURST
THE NATIONAL CONSERVATIVE CANDIDATE

to

Dumble's Election Address, 1945

challenging, and through which he would have had more contact with kindred spirits. I found one as I reached my early thirties – politics. This appeared in my life through supporting my friend Mike Waterhouse in his parliamentary candidacy in Leicester, a constituency once represented for decades by his eminent grandfather, Deputy Chief Whip and later leading Suez rebel, Captain Charles Waterhouse. I knew immediately I had found my niche. Local party officials saw it too and encouraged me to have a go.

Politics for me was a welcome relief from years of dabbling in business, all the time knowing in my heart that I would never be a businessman. As I later used to tell bemused Bolton school groups visiting Parliament who enquired after my motives for entering politics, it had mainly served to get my parents off my back. This had the advantage of being true.

For Dumble it could have been a natural progression. His father Buck had had a long and distinguished political career, and he had been brought up surrounded by political cronies. It is hard to believe that having stood in the khaki election of 1945 as the Conservative candidate for a solidly socialist East End seat Bethnal Green, pictured on a public platform with Winston beside him, that he had entirely escaped the political bug. Indeed, in 1946 he became chairman of the London Young Conservatives. This was not a move indicative of a young man with no thoughts of a political career.

A chance presented itself in the early 1950s. The then safe seat of Hastings needed a candidate, and perhaps as a result of local family connections, it was suggested that if Dumble showed an interest,

Campaigning with Winston in Bethnal Green 1945

he stood a good chance of becoming the MP. According to the official view, this was impractical on grounds of his not being a barrister, which was seen as the only profession which allowed someone of moderate means the luxury of a political career. I never bought this. The Sackvilles had managed to live for centuries well above their means, and I did not see my grandparents as exactly destitute. A way could have been found.

The real stumbling block was undoubtedly at home. Early involvement with the world of politics can act as a deterrent rather than a magnet. Poppy's mother Joan, despite being the niece of a Liberal Prime Minister, had become inextricably bound up with local Conservative Party affairs, reaching the dizzy heights of chairman of the Maidstone Conservative Association. But constituency politics involved then as now endless committee meetings, chaired by self-important Captain Mainwarings or their female equivalents, wine and cheese fundraisers and endless parochial gossip. All of which was anathema to my mother, a far cry from the glamorous, brilliant future she imagined for herself. Becoming an MP's wife would have looked like a step back not forward.

In 1954, Joan had a brush with destiny. There was a vacancy for a candidate for Maidstone following the impending retirement of Alfred Bossom, MP, of whom Churchill once observed, 'Odd sort of name – neither one thing nor the other.' The short list was published. It included one Margaret Hilda Roberts. But she was rejected as a candidate, allegedly vetoed by Joan, who judged her to be 'too pretty'. This probably masked the well-known preference of Tory women for being represented by a male, and in those days a male of a certain background. But as we now know, Miss Roberts – who never in her whole life admitted defeat – went on to find a better seat in North London, finally becoming not just Prime Minister but arguably the most powerful woman in the world, friend and ally of Reagan and Gorbachev, and a key player in ending the Cold War.

Politics might have provided Dumble with the vocation he needed, as well as a source of solace and fascination. He was good with people, would have been a conscientious constituency MP and happy to be part of an eccentric club, the House of Commons. He would have had difficulty deciding whether he inclined more to the Whig or Tory persuasion. He was moreover a natural rebel and would have taken up positions of principle before advantage. None of which would have propelled him up the greasy pole, but he would not have minded and might even have resisted the temptation to seek ministerial office.

I used to do a semi-humorous talk on what qualifies you for politics. First, a dominating or jealousy-inspiring sibling. His brother Harry had by all accounts the charisma and star quality Dumble lacked. Second, a shortage of parental affection. My grandparents were very social in addition to Buck's string of not very discreet romantic liaisons. And of course politicians are obsessed with themselves and their political careers to the exclusion of all else, which may explain why their children have a habit of going a bit wonky. Third, a lack of social success in those vital teenage years, especially in the closing minutes of teenage dances. I have the feeling that Dumble scored quite highly on all three. The spurious notoriety that comes with being an MP might have been just what the doctor ordered.

In politics, if you are not interested in or amused by the ongoing saga, your spouse's career amounts to little more than an isolating, boring distraction from the family. Even if you are, your lack of a voice can be deeply frustrating, especially if you are the brighter of the two. Sasha Swire's recently published mischievous diary about the vagaries of her husband Hugo's career says it all. For whatever reason, maybe a combination of several, Dumble did not put himself forward for Hastings and persisted with his labours for British industry.

While unspectacular, these were far from unsuccessful. British Election Traction moved on from being a bus and tram operator to become an early British example of an industrial conglomerate, a holding company with fingers in many pies.

Newly appointed bus manager in East Yorks 1957

*Dumble qualified as a bus driver – he insisted on being
capable of doing whatever his employees had to*

Post-war forced nationalisations provided a cash
pile, enabling it to diversify by acquiring numer-
ous other assets. These included Wembley Stadium,
regional newspapers, Thames Television, maga-
zines, laundries, waste management, construction
and plant hire. Dumble found himself involved in

a whole series of disparate businesses, from the Midland Red Bus Company to Dreamland, the famous funfair (today 'theme park') in the then unfashionable Kent riviera resort of Margate.

But his career really blossomed within the media subsidiary Rediffusion, pioneer in the distribution (as opposed to content) of radio and television through a wired relay network, the purest example of 'cable TV'. The concept was simple: you put up a tall aerial outside a centre of population, often a 'new town' and charge a simple rent per house for a screen and access to signals piped in from a wire running down the street. You can even shut off supply from outside the property if the subscribers fail to pay. Until rendered obsolete by new technologies, this was how millions of British people got their telly, especially in the North and the new towns. Organising all this, often as the monopoly provider, involved negotiations with local councils' community leaders. Given Dumble's generally centrifugal attitude to life, this was right up his alley. He was justly proud of his achievements, and earned the loyalty and respect of those who worked for him.

I sometimes accompanied him on business trips. One involved the mining town of Wombwell in Nottinghamshire. The afternoon entertainment included a visit to a deep mine, crawling along a constantly advancing 26-foot-high seam hundreds of feet underground, coal cutters roaring ahead of us, the ceiling falling in behind. I barely kept my claustrophobia under control. Years later, at the time of the miners' strike, as one of Mrs Thatcher's new MPs and potentially under fire, I lost relatively little sleep over mine closures. If we could find a way to satisfy our energy needs without sending men day after day, year after year down into the Dantesque hell I had briefly experienced, it was progress.

The coal mine was followed by a trip, at my request, to a nearby village to pay homage outside the house where D.H. Lawrence was born. *Sons and Lovers* was my set text for O-level English. We then proceeded to a local comprehensive where Dumble gave an inspired address to hundreds of children, charming them by gently ribbing the Head and members of staff. Dumble at his very best.

This trip was sadly memorable for its rarity. There were few family outings, perhaps because my parents had such differing tastes. An exception was in 1964, when Dumble acquired through his business four precious tickets to the Beatles Christmas Show at Hammersmith Odeon. In those days, you got a whole programme for your money. In addition to the star turn, there were warm-ups from Freddie and the Dreamers, Sounds Incorporated, Elkie Brooks and the Yardbirds, to name but a few. As an aspiring rocker and member of a rather dire school band, I was in clover just hearing the Yardbirds' live rendition of 'Gloria'.

When they finally appeared, the Fab Four were a slight let-down. Inadequate amplification typical of those early days rendered their whole set inaudible against the hysterical screaming of the mainly female teenage audience. I did however greatly enjoy the spectacle of massed waves of mini-skirted girls charging the stage, ineffectively repelled by the apologies for bouncers. My mother, perusing the chaotic events below through a pair of Victorian opera glasses, was heard to exclaim, 'My God, isn't that Emma Soames?'

Dumble's career was noble and worthy but rarely glamorous. Poppy just never understood it. She told of a busman's dinner she had attended in the Midlands: coming from her this could have meant any point on the map from north of the Park to the southern border of Aberdeenshire. There had clearly been no meeting of minds. I never heard of her attending any more such occasions.

Things looked up a bit when Dumble was put in charge of Rediffusion's external broadcasting operations, covering various far-flung parts of the Empire. As these included the English-speaking Caribbean, my mother became noticeably less reluctant to play the supportive wife. During Dumble's annual tours, she was happy to install herself at the then still genteel Sandy Lane in Barbados. When Kingston or Georgetown beckoned, he was left to get on with it on his own.

Running the Jamaican business in particular

In charge of broadcasting in Jamaica c.1960

was no picnic. Elections were not quite like the rather sedate British affairs on which they were supposedly modelled. In some areas, candidates armed their supporters with handguns to protect themselves or impress their political opponents. For one election, Dumble was tasked to get on the right side of the successful Prime Ministerial candidate to ensure the continuity of the Rediffusion franchise. Unable to make up his mind (a family failing), he made financial arrangements with both. This ostensibly sensible plan got out to the press and became a scandal, causing much heartache and guilt for its author. Quite separately, his local (British) manager got loose in the rum houses of Kingston, committing squalid acts which on exposure necessitated his removal. All this caused Dumble, who always hated giving anyone bad news, even more pain and led to another episode then erroneously referred to as a nervous breakdown.

Poppy also had little hesitation in supporting him on trips to Malta, where our cousin Mable Maitland entertained in style on her yacht in the famous Valletta harbour. Less cordial were relations with the anti-colonial firebrand leader of Malta, Dom Mintoff. Rediffusion's broadcasting operation was one day unceremoniously expropriated in the name of media nationalisation. There was nothing Dumble or anyone could do about it.

Thanks to parent company BET's ownership of Wembley, they were expected to attend the most important footballing event of the year, the FA Cup Final, an invitation which even Poppy, an untypical football supporter, was delighted to accept. The attraction for Poppy was that she was generally seated next to the Prime Minister of the day. Despite her lack of enthusiasm for matters provincial, like most women, Poppy found Mr Wilson's blunt pipe-smoking Yorkshire manner (theatrical though it may have been) beguiling. She liked to inform such a political audience that she was a Radical. Having never shown interest in that great movement's traditional aims, universal suffrage and the condition of the working class, it is hard to say what she thought she meant by the term. Nevertheless, it was an approach that seems to have proved fit for purpose, and she and Wilson got on like a house on fire.

Around that time there was a sad little incident, which encapsulates the difficulties of their marriage and the wide gulf between them. One evening, Dumble arrived back from the office with important news, brimming with pride. He had been asked to step up to the top job – managing director of Rediffusion. Poppy's reaction was not as he would have hoped and included the words 'surely people like us become chairman'. One can see what she meant, but it once again demonstrated her lack of empathy with Dumble's whole life plan. To use the modern expression, she just did not get it.

7

Dumble did in the end have a political career of a sort. On the death of his father in 1976 and his own retirement from Rediffusion, he took his seat in the Lords. He immersed himself in the controversies of the day, becoming a disciple of Jim Prior, the left-leaning Secretary of State for Employment in the new 1979 Tory government. Prior was seeking to apply the brakes to Mrs T's radical plans for curbing the trade unions' ability to further damage British industry, thus becoming de facto leader of the 'wets' in her party. Dumble was politically guilty by association.

She had reason to be suspicious of the Tory toffs. They had a nasty habit of letting her down. After only a couple of years in office, she could not count on the support of many of the old guard. Soames, Carrington and Gilmour were among those who had become discomfited by her frontal assault on collectivist ideas, which offended their paternalistic view of how grand people should govern. They had a habit of sniggering about what they saw as the Poujadiste shopkeeper's daughter behind her back.

Dumble was probably tarred by the same brush. Where he felt strongly about something the government was getting wrong, he did not feel constrained by the mere fact of taking the Conservative whip, and his attitude to the Falklands campaign was especially likely to upset the occupant of No. 10.

A highlight of his career in the Lords was being invited to introduce to membership the great Harold Macmillan, who Mrs Thatcher had created a hereditary (rare honour then, unthinkable today) peer, to be known as Earl of Stockton, an event immortalised on the cover of *Private Eye*. Although a towering figure in her youth, SuperMac must have been far from being one of her political heroes. He was remembered for trashing the rules on control of the money supply while in office – later a central plank of her economic policy – provoking the resignation of his entire treasury team.

He also accelerated the independence of many parts of the Empire, with often dire consequences for the subjects of those nations from their new leaders. He also boasted of having built huge numbers of new homes, most of them now remembered more as ill-fated concrete tower-block estates.

Macmillan was also, depending on who you believe, the *éminence grise* behind the last-minute withdrawal of the Anglo-French-Israeli forces from the Suez Canal Zone in the midst of the campaign of 1956, bringing national humiliation for Britain and a disastrous propaganda boost for the wrong kind of Arab nationalism. It may have been politically unavoidable, but Macmillan's intervention in predicting financial meltdown if we went ahead had the predicable effect of forcing the increasingly unwell and embattled Anthony Eden out of office, and propelling himself into No. 10.

Decades later, Macmillan entertained their Lordships by wittily describing the greatest Thatcher policy of all, privatisation of the moribund, unproductive, union-dominated state enterprises assets such as electricity, water and telecommunications as 'selling off the family silver'. Maybe he was by then detached enough to believe these really should remain as state monopolies. But more likely his widely reported remarks were merely a chance for a cheap dig at the simplistic policies of the 'shopkeeper's daughter'.

In any case, his critics were quick to point out

Introducing Harold
Macmillan as a member
of the House of Lords

that they also served to reinforce the improbable
notion that the Macmillans had any family silver.

What has this got to do with the subject of this
memoir? Just that taken together with his sogginess
on trade-union policy, the Falklands and to name
but a few aspects of Dumble's political activity, he
did little to endear himself to Margaret Thatcher.
He had a rebellious, anti-authoritarian streak and
would have reacted badly to the schoolmarm aspects
of her style of government, while hugely admiring
her courage and extraordinary achievements.

I shared, or perhaps inherited from him, the same
career-limiting perversity. One evening 'in the lob-
bies' I had persuaded my friend Mark Lennox-Boyd,
then her PPS, to set up an encounter with the PM.
As a north-west MP, I was an enthusiastic supporter
of Manchester Airport, which I saw as an economic

powerhouse for the whole region. I therefore had strong views about the fate of the collapsed domestic operator, British Caledonian. I was convinced that the best way of ensuring the vitally needed direct services out of Manchester across the Atlantic and to the Far East and Australasia was by bringing in a fresh operator to create a genuine 'hub'. If BA was allowed to gobble up Caledonian they would continue to ferry northern passengers down to Heathrow to connect with their long-haul flights.

Another bidder, the Scandinavian airline SAS, was promising direct routes and new planes – in fact most of what we wanted. My appeal to the PM, carefully rehearsed, was that she at least allow referral of BA's bid to the Monopolies Commission and let them decide. She fired back with, 'Your colleagues do not appear to agree with you.'

Irritated by her unwillingness to tackle the argument on its merits, I took a dangerous tack. I suggested that out of some 350 Tory 'colleagues' at least 200 had received free upgrades from BA, even to go on holiday with their families. The Prime Minister said nothing, spun on her heel like a prima ballerina and was off. Impugning the methods of her hero, the chairman of BA, Lord King, the architect of one of the first great privatisations and creator of the 'world's favourite airline', was not the best route to preferment.

This tendency to challenge established orthodoxies, in ways which might well play to his disadvantage, was a central part of Dumble's character. In keeping with his own military career, the regimental pecking order was something about which he clearly held strong beliefs, and he did not care who heard them.

At a dinner party at Spye with Aunt Avice, a discussion of military matters took place between him and other guests, including an eminent retired general. Dumble announced that in his view regiments should be called by numbers, rather than bear names reminiscent of royal personages or past glories. This went down extremely badly with the Queen Mother, who was also present and was of course colonel-in-chief of several historic regiments. It also appalled the rest of the company, who would have disapproved of anyone they knew holding such opinions, as they would the airing of any opinion which displeased a senior royal.

I do not however want to leave an impression that my father was unpatriotic, a pacifist like his father or in any way against the military. Quite the reverse. He set great store by his NATO activities and was a great admirer of generals, especially those blessed with a brain.

Indeed, he believed fervently in the benefits of military training for young people. In his middle years, he became an avid supporter of the Sussex Army Cadet Force, within which he was given honorary rank and acquired a smart uniform, albeit on the tight-fitting side. I remember tense moments worrying whether he was going to be able to squeeze into it for some upcoming military occasion. His interest in part-time military service was one of his more enduring voluntary pursuits. He was honorary colonel of the cadets for over fifteen years. Likewise, he was a long-serving chairman of the Sussex Playing Fields Association.

Another interest was osteopathy. He served as President of the General Council of Osteopaths. Luckily, we never discussed my strongly sceptical view of alternative and complimentary medicines generally. After his death, I was tasked as a Health Minister to introduce a Bill to Parliament giving the profession of osteopath protected status for the first time, and for his sake, despite my personal feelings, I was proud to do so.

What Dumble actually said of his life in the Lords was that he would rather die than be 'back in harness'. After years of struggling up the rather rickety corporate ladder, who could blame him for now shunning the greasy pole? The life of a junior minister in the Lords or spokesman for a government department is not especially satisfying. Having attended many ministerial meetings over the years, I cannot help noticing that whichever minister was doing the business in the Lords was hardly central to policymaking and only rarely taken seriously. My friend and patron in the Whips Office Tristan Garel-Jones, with whom I shared Spanish connections, used to refer dismissively to Lords ministers as 'Binkies'. Like many politicos however, he was at the same time somewhat in awe of them.

Perhaps as a result of remaining as a back-bencher and keeping his independence, Dumble loved the place. On my rare visits, I was amazed by how many peers of all parties he stopped to chat with. It was then a great club, full of distinguished members, already a large proportion there on merit and appointment, not by birth. Members moved around at a stately pace on arthritic joints expressing portentous civilities to each other the while. It was the polar opposite of the nasty, confrontational bear pit down the passage of which I was a member. As well as a rather highbrow social life, it provided a forum in which to calmly discuss, and sometimes even influence, the great issues of the day.

8

Dumble's role as a 'working peer', and in particular, serving on a sub-committee of NATO (an organisation which goes through the motions of parliamentary oversight) was the source of much satisfaction to him – and to Poppy. It marked a new happier stage in their lives together. For the first time, they were on the same page, pursuing activities of mutual interest, including elaborate VIP trips as guests of foreign and often exotic

*Dumble on first visit to the State of Delaware,
with Lt Governor and Mrs Dupont*

governments. One NATO meeting in Turkey was
memorable for the delegation members, lunching
on the balcony of their hotel, being treated to the
sight of the Soviet Black Sea fleet at close quarters,
steaming down the Bosphorus in a stately display
of defiance. Moscow may have slightly overesti-
mated the influence on Western policy exerted by
the watching politicians, or perhaps just needed

an opportunity to give their old tubs a spin, but it made Poppy and Dumble's day.

They got invitations to exciting events around the world, like the Paris Air Show. US plane maker Northrop clearly knew how to get the attention of celebrity guests. Dumble and Poppy were driven in a large car from their hotel in Paris out to Le Bourget, escorted by motorcycle outriders. For years later, I never ceased to marvel at the ingenuity with which Poppy found opportunities to tell this story, sometimes even to bemused strangers encountered in shops.

The presidential inauguration ball was another. It was never clear to me how they infiltrated the Reagan circle so effectively. It may have been through their old friends the Fairbanks family, who were close to US Ambassador Walter Annenberg, his wife Lee and other members of the 'kitchen cabinet'. But there they were, dancing the night away in some of the glitziest scenes Washington had witnessed for years. There were also jolly times in Palm Springs, mingling with such Hollywood legends as Jimmy Stewart, and in Rome with Bill Wilson, long time Reagan backer and later Ambassador to the Holy See.

Another US connection was the state of Delaware (sic), named after the river in the mouth of which a seventeenth-century Lord De La Warr had been shipwrecked on the way to Virginia, of which he was governor. Tiny state though it is, it

Poppy in Palm Beach with Douglas
Fairbanks and Laurence Olivier

provides much appreciated tax advantages today
to many US corporate entities. De La Warr was
head of the ancient West family, who later brought
their earldom to the Sackvilles through marriage.
By luck, the state's (Republican) senator, Bill Roth,
was a fellow member of the NATO Council, and
Dumble and he became firm friends. Bill and his
wife Jane, later to become an appeal court judge,
suffered from constant problems with the more
recently elected fellow senator from Delaware, one
Joe Biden, a Democrat. Bill and Jane nursed a deep
loathing for Biden, about which on their visits to
Buckhurst they became surprisingly vocal and
specific. Dumble and Poppy were several times

guests of the state, a celebrity role they found not uncongenial.

Through various channels came other interesting international liaisons. Dumble did business with the giant South African conglomerate Barlow Rand, of whom Rediffusion was local joint venture partner. Chairman Mike Rosholt and his wife became friends, and introduced Dumble and Poppy to the delights of Sandton society. The South African government still suffered from a degree of pariah status, as a result of its continuing apartheid policies, and was split on how rapidly it should be pursuing the majority rule which the rest of the world was pushing at them, and which more realistic white South Africans knew to be inevitable.

Dumble, always more of a patrician than an ideological conservative, was unsurprisingly drawn towards the liberal wing of South African politics. He was befriended by the long serving Foreign Minister, Pik Botha, who was to the left of his party and from time to time slapped down by his leader for statements favouring an end to white rule. Dumble was recruited as an unofficial ambassador for the business community and the more flexible faction of the ruling National Party. Britain was rightly seen as an important ally for South Africa, in view of the pressure from around the world for economic sanctions, resisted by Margaret Thatcher on the grounds that they would most damage the poorest South Africans.

Dumble made another important friendship. Sharp-eyed observers at the time may have spotted him driving one Mangosuthu Buthelezi to meetings around Westminster and St James's. The earl and the hereditary Zulu chieftain, neither of them small men, competing for space in the front of Dumble's already pokey Ford Escort must have been an unusual sight. In offering his diplomatic and chauffeuring assistance, my father clearly recognised Buthelezi as a remarkable figure, accepted by the white government as head of the four-million-strong KwaZulu 'homeland' and leader of the Inkatha political party. He later served the new government as Minister of Home Affairs.

Buthelezi had his critics: he implicitly supported the 'homeland' policy. But he steered a skilful middle path in challenging the more extreme aspects of the ANC, accepting 'self-government' for his Zulu subjects while rejecting the clearly bogus independence offered to and adopted by some other 'homelands'. His narrow regional and ethnic support base would always have made his ambitions for national leadership difficult: in any case no one could have come anywhere within reach of the great unifier Nelson Mandela. But Buthelezi took good advantage of his tribal position to play a role in the events which led to South Africa confounding the cynics to become the Rainbow Nation it remains today.

Other perambulations resulted from their

energetic activity on the embassy cocktail circuit. Poppy and Dumble befriended the Chinese ambassador. With early 1980s Anglo-Chinese relations not as warm as they were to be later and the Bamboo Curtain still opaque, the Chinese found an active member of the Lords taking an interest in their country's affairs worth encouraging. On more than one occasion, Dumble and Poppy found themselves in Beijing as slightly improbable guests of the Chinese Communist Party. Likewise, they became close to the Philippine ambassador. On their visit to Manila, sadly Imelda Marcos – with whom a meeting was scheduled – became suddenly unavailable, but Poppy was granted a glimpse of the shoes.

9

It might sound as though Dumble, on arriving at his sixties and retirement, could look back with some satisfaction on a varied life, during which he could count significant achievements. But that was not how his mind worked. He was never going to luxuriate in the self-congratulation you see in some people at that stage in their lives, even beforehand in too many cases. He had unfinished business and never stopped looking for some objective he was never likely to reach.

Nothing went right from the early to mid 1980s

to his death in 1988. There tends to be more than one reason why someone is driven to do something so dramatic and final as to take his own life. Family and close friends make the mistake of looking in vain for a single cause, often blaming themselves at the same time. In reality, the descent to total despair is more likely to be cumulative, gradual and, to use the modern expression, multi-factorial.

Dumble was not happy in his own skin. He was never the slim, athletic, self-confident figure to which he aspired. He was short and dumpy, and he minded. But he had the courage to make light of it. He liked to quote David Cecil's description of the young Melbourne: 'Handsome, verging to

Poppy in Beijing, c. 1980

portly.' He made huge efforts to control his weight, but everything about his lifestyle militated against these. To control weight, you generally need to start by limiting your intake of starches and sugars, in his case particularly rich French food and alcohol.

People often think they can make some progress with sustained, vigorous exercise, but the exertion needed goes way beyond what most people could contemplate or their busy lives can accommodate. At weekends, Dumble had titanic struggles on the tennis court, if a willing partner could be found. Although my sister Arabella's marriage ended badly, Dumble was for a time lucky in his son-in-law, city banker Giovanni Emo di Capodilista. Although a vastly better player, Giovanni clearly saw it as his duty to spend hours pulling his punches, ensuring that his father-in-law ended up exhausted by long exchanges across the net, and sometimes even allowed him to win. Exasperatingly, Giovanni was able to follow this up in the evening, though not a native English speaker, by effortlessly trouncing us all at Scrabble.

Other attempts at weight loss were more dramatic. Dumble favoured Herculean struggles with nature, decimating an overgrown shrubbery or thinning woodland. I remember one Saturday evening, darkness had fallen and dinner time was approaching, but there was no sign of him. He had been last seen heading in the direction of the lake with a barrowload of saws and other fearsome instruments. A search party equipped with torches was quickly assembled. It did not take long to find him. He had lain trapped for several hours, pinned down by a tree which had apparently retaliated by falling in an unforeseen direction. Several of his ribs were broken, leaving him unable to move or emit more than low moans. Somehow the errant tree was shifted sufficiently to drag him from under it. He was borne on a make-do stretcher to the house, where the family doctor pronounced him lucky to be alive.

I reached the conclusion over the years that Dumble was trying to lose himself in these obsessive endeavours and find some alleviation from all his worries and doubts, what some people might call his demons. His efforts with an axe were reminiscent of that disturbing scene in *Lawrence of Arabia* where 'our hero' takes revenge on the Turkish army.

One of his fundamental problems was that he did not seem to have close or lasting friendships. His best man was a childhood friend, Tom Fairfax, but I do not recall Fairfax ever playing a role in his later life. Most people have at least a few best buddies, whether from childhood, school, university, work or extended family. These are people with whom we can get together over a drink, or on the telephone, and exchange confidences. Dumble did not appear to have any such confidantes. An important source for most people was denied to him, that is three years at university, from which I think he would have greatly benefited. Mainly thanks to the war, he never got that chance and failed to link up with intelligent contemporaries.

Neither my brother or I were close to him, and rarely if ever were we taken into his confidence. I probably had more in common with him than William. I appear however to have inherited some of his personality traits. We both found ourselves more at home with relative strangers, people with whom we had been thrown together, than we did with those with whom we had been brought up. We were both ill-equipped to do justice to cock-tail parties, dances and weekends in the country. It sounds paradoxical, but tacitly understanding a lot about each other made us less rather than more likely to discuss it. Typically British.

My sister Arabella, born seven years after me, was another matter. He doted on her, they had a close rapport and he called her 'Duddy'. Arabella was an attractive child, with blonde curly hair and a slightly ethereal quality about her. I remember their sessions at the weighing scales, with Dumble alternately praised and reprimanded for the ups and downs in his weight. In her late teens, Arabella had some success as a model and featured in advertising campaigns for some well-known products, of which Oil of Ulay (now Olay) sticks in my memory.

It became apparent later that he had given Arabella a number of properties on the estate,

Arabella with Giovanni, flanked by
Best Man and another supporter

eventually valued for probate at several million pounds. This did not worry me greatly, as I (rather unwisely) affected in those days to be above acquisitive behaviour and therefore had few expectations. But such generosity to his daughter never went down well with other members of the family.

Sadly, Arabella was not well equipped to deal with adulthood and marriage. This may have been the result of a subconscious desire to continue as the spoilt child, or even the longer term effects of an incident when, as a baby, she became suddenly and dangerously dehydrated: her life was only saved by being driven at breakneck speed to hospital by the local GP.

I now regret having failed to prevent her (in

Arabella with "Stevie" her
(previously my) former governess

hindsight I could have forced a 'deadlock' sale) from buying me out and taking over the management of a rather run-down pub we had jointly inherited near Buckhurst. Arabella seemed to have found her vocation and looked quite at home behind the bar. But picking at a chicken in the basket in the pub failed to satisfy the life expectations of her jet-setting husband. Her new role, combined with a refusal to have children, must have contributed to his decision to throw in the towel. Giovanni departed permanently for London, where he eventually married a more predictable lady of European origin.

Following her acrimonious divorce, Arabella went steadily downhill. She took to spending afternoons as well as lunches at the pub in the company of some of the hardened local drinkers. Within a few months, she was complaining of swollen ankles: a hepatologist diagnosed rapidly advancing cirrhosis, likely to be fatal within six months.

Arabella took immediate action but with characteristic obstinacy failed to follow the important advice, which I assume she was offered, on how to reverse alcohol addiction. Far from having herself being admitted for detox under medical supervision facilitated by tranquilisers and going into therapy, Arabella just stopped drinking. The shock to her system led to a serious stroke, leaving her hospitalised, finally unable to walk unaided. A further stroke left her unable to form a sentence or make herself understood other than to her companion, John Gramolt, who still looks after her at her home near Buckhurst.

By this time, Dumble had already left us. He was spared the tragedy of her disablement but had undoubtedly begun to worry about the direction her life was taking. It was naturally a ghastly shock for the rest of the family but most of all for my mother, one she bore with her usual tight-lipped fortitude. Watching her daughter's decline, and the ruin of all her hopes and dreams for her, must have been a torment, one that endured for the rest of her life.

10

So who did Dumble really confide in? As mentioned above, people he worked with in various

Dumble preoccupied c. 1975

capacities. First his lawyers, originally two senior partners of the renowned family trust specialists Macfarlanes. They were replaced by a younger partner, John Rhodes. According to my mother, who spoke of Dumble's dealings with Macfarlanes as though she would rather he spent his time consulting the Kray brothers, he paid out prodigious fees for ever more exotic tax schemes to reduce liabilities on an estate rapidly diminishing in value.

And of course he also spent far too much time

with his doctors, persuading them to refer him to specialists for conditions which were entirely in his imagination. Though overweight, he was never to my knowledge definably ill. He was a hypochondriac and seemed proud of it, prone to boasting of being able to identify dozens of pills at a glance. He was someone who, as the old joke goes, 'enjoyed poor health… enjoyed it enormously'. He had even more frequent sessions with psychiatrists, baring his soul in return for ever more alarming combinations of drugs which arguably did not help him and were a major cause of his untimely death.

He was similarly close to people he met through work. Warren Clewlow was the 'bright young man' originally assigned by Rediffusion's South African partner Barlow Rand to look after Dumble and Poppy on their many visits to South Africa. Warren became a close friend. He eventually became a long-serving CEO of Barlow Rand, I like to think aided by guidance and encouragement from Dumble, who, as he once told me, was like a father to him.

Another serious gap in Dumble's life was any real contact with the rest of his family. He had no close cousins, had lost his brother Harry, and only rarely saw his sister, latterly known as Kitty Giles. Despite her being nearly five years his junior, he shared with her not only genes, but the same quirky and questioning approach. I fear that Dumble missed out on much by not being part of her life. The worlds she moved in were full of the kind of bright, high achievers he might well have found more entertaining than the pleasant but essentially *ancien régime* types he often found himself hosting at Buckhurst.

I always put their apparent estrangement down to Poppy having nothing in common with her and effectively excommunicating her from his life. I regret that I have few memories of the Giles family from that time, beyond the occasions we all met up with my grandparents at Fishers Gate and their annual visits to us for Christmas tea.

These were somewhat sticky occasions, but on one occasion enlivened when Dumble mounted a rickety stepladder to light the candles on our Christmas tree. It was a considerable specimen: we had high ceilings, and my parents liked to acquire a tree which would take advantage of every available inch. As we sat down, there was a terrible crash from the other end of the hall. We realised that Dumble had lost his balance, perhaps insufficiently recovered from a magnificent lunch, grabbed the tree and disappeared under a rapidly developing funeral pyre. Swift action was taken and disaster averted, but had the tree not been green and recently cut, there could have been a serious conflagration. I sometimes wondered if such incidents were in fact stunts pulled by Dumble for the entertainment of his extended family.

My aunt Kitty, as I later realised, was a remarkable figure. On top of her very active social life, she worked hard to ease the burdens of the most disadvantaged. This was not just talk, as with so many well-meaning people. She put it into practice. Her focus was the penal system. For over half a century, she volunteered as a visitor at HM Prison Brixton. She also served time on the parole board.

Her memorial service at Brixton was a great affair. I remember arriving on a cold, sunny day and coming across a queue of folk unusually elegantly attired for prison visiting. It appeared to be as difficult to get in as to break out. The service included moving addresses from the chaplain, with whom she was clearly close, the governor and others. Widely known as 'Lady Kitty', she was a legend in the South London prison world and treated with great respect, especially by those governors who did not follow her advice to the letter. Towards the end of the ensuing lunch, I noticed that the person I was chatting to was loading a paper bag with food from the buffet. I asked why. 'Taking them back to my cell for later, ain't I.'

Kitty was also a great figure in the Ionians, in the early 1970s following in the footsteps of the Durrells to Corfu. In fact, Kitty's interest in Corfu dated back to touring the islands as long ago as the 1950s on the Niarchos yacht, falling in love with Corfu on sight. She first took a house near the Old Town, a tumbling-down Venetian villa belonging to local Count Palatiano, perhaps a real version of what BBC stylists mocked up for their latest recent Durrell series.

As cousin Belinda recalls from her childhood:

> I remember several years of tramping over the rocks in the northeast of the island looking for the right spot. We later on stayed in relative comfort with my sister's godmother Baba Metcalfe, but every day we would set off to meet farmers wanting to sell us their stremma of land.

Eventually Kitty came across the tiny fishing village of Άγιος Στέφανος – or San Stefano as we visitors call it. There in 1970, they bought enough land to build the charming Villa Katerina, on a promontory overlooking the harbour, with its own private mooring below. She chose well. The view from the balcony on which they entertained their many guests matched any on the island, stretching for miles back to Corfu Town with its unmistakable silhouettes of the two Venetian forts guarding the harbour, a view often captured in the sketches of the great Edward Lear.

Meanwhile, San Stefano under Kitty's beady eye survived as an unspoilt jewel of an Ionian village, with its ring of tavernas and shops around the bay. Villa Katerina was built in the days when material had to come by boat and donkey, by Kostas, the father of Nikos, owner of the well-known Taverna Galini, still the favoured lunch venue of discerning

*Dumble's sister Kitty Giles in Corfu, with clearly
post–prandial son Sebastian and nephew Tom*

local Brits. It is no surprise that Kitty earned the
title, bestowed without sarcasm but with real affection, of Queen of Corfu. She spoke Greek and was
a beloved friend of the whole community.

In all she did, Kitty was supported by her eru-
dite, diligent and hard-working husband, Frank,
who she had met in those momentous months of
late 1944 in Paris, where he was the eager young
Paris correspondent of *The Times*. Kitty was at the
British Embassy, an unpaid lady-in-waiting to her
friend, the legendary ambassadress and nominally
ducal daughter Lady Diana Cooper. Ambassador
Duff Cooper had been one of Churchill's closest
political allies. Before the war, he had been a prominent anti-appeaser and, as already mentioned, to
his credit actually resigned over Munich.

Frank went on to ever great things, rising inexorably up the ladder at Times Newspapers, in 1981 becoming editor of *The Sunday Times*. His critics alleged that while highly capable, he was more pedantic than inspired. Certainly Frank had that side to him, peppering his discourse with French epithets. My maternal grandfather Geoffrey Devas, following a lecture on the qualities of the wine during one Christmas lunch, took him aside to inform him that, 'Frank, in our day we just had good wine.' But anyone who gets right to the top of their profession without being a bully or machinator (he was neither) deserves huge respect. Frank was a consummate professional. He clearly knew as much as anyone about getting a quality newspaper out onto the street.

Unfortunately, in 1983 he was caught in the flak from the Hitler Diaries scandal, an event which ended his career. It had all resulted from the foolish behaviour of a group of powerful egos, including Murdoch, the new owner of *The Times*, and Axel Springer of *Stern*. Meanwhile, Professor Trevor-Roper, historian and Times board member, claimed to have the necessary expertise to authenticate the material, which it turned out he clearly did not. They were all dazzled into thinking the patently improbable diaries were the journalistic find of the century. During the week preceding publication, with doubts growing, there was panic in Murdoch's office that *Newsweek*, who had negotiated the US rights, was going to break ranks, scooping the story worldwide. Days before publication, Frank found that Murdoch had decided to switch publication from *The Times*, whose staff had up to then owned the story, to the edition of *The Sunday Times* due out in three days' time. Frank and his team had no chance to apply normal journalistic checks. They were just told to publish.

The only evasive action available to Frank, with the main pages already set and the presses about to roll, was to walk out. But such a course would have required this conservative and prudent man to abandon his loyal staff, some of whom he had known for thirty years, give up the considerable prestige of his position as editor and, one assumes, a substantial pension. He stayed, and the whole fiasco erupted around him. Heads rolled, including his own and those of his colleagues, but not of course that of Murdoch, who simply boasted of having increased the sales of his newspapers.

Frank and Kitty had made many interesting and talented friends. Paris was full of influential American and British officials, posted there after the liberation to plan and administer the Marshall Plan and the reconstruction of European democracy. When I arrived in New York in the early 1970s, I was invited to a party given in their honour by old friend Nin Ryan, heiress of a fortune from her father, the Kuhn, Loeb & Co. banker and philanthropist Otto Kahn. The great and good were there, from media moguls to the mayor to patrons of the arts. I had difficulty preventing one Mary Scott, who I had brought with me, from leaving the party with a very persistent Henry Kissinger. I later understood why friends at work insisted on calling her 'Mary, Scott of Queens' and wished I had not prevented the eminent lothario from having his wicked way.

My mother's behaviour to her sister-in-law Kitty left a lot to be desired, swinging between hostile and glacial. Poppy excelled at glacial and could turn a great cold shoulder. If she had put her mind to it, she could have put global warming on hold. On the other hand, Kitty showed little aptitude for appeasement or understanding of the nature of her adversary. Things had been bad from the start. Back in 1945, Poppy had set a date on which her engagement was to be announced. When the day dawned, Kitty was gone. It transpired she was heading north, with a Canadian airman billeted at Buckhurst with whom she had taken up. Buck set out in pursuit, catching up with them in Liverpool, where Kitty was finally persuaded to return home. Poppy was convinced that the whole episode had little to do with the attractions of the Canadian but was rather a well-aimed shot at spoiling her big day.

It may also be that it was also Dumble's own decision to distance himself from his sister, for a number of reasons. One is the traumatic loss of their brother Harry and its effect on his attitude to his surviving sibling. Shared grief can drive people apart, instead of bringing them together as it should. It is said the marriages of those who have to endure the agony of the loss of a child often do not survive.

Another possibility is that Dumble did not entirely approve of Kitty's liberal lifestyle: he was conscious of the odder aspects of his childhood and her influences from the eccentricities of the preceding generations, and was not comfortable with either. He may have felt the need of a straight-as-a-die establishmentarianist like Poppy to drag him back to normality.

11

I hope that Dumble was at least somewhat fulfilled by his business career and had a few laughs during his time at the office. For a quarter of a century, he and Poppy did not see much of each other, because while he was dining and sleeping in Sussex, he was spending most of his waking hours in London, or commuting to and fro. I don't want to make too much of this: I realise he was hardly alone as victim of this tyranny: before Covid intervened, an estimated one million people made the daily journey from outside London into the Square Mile alone.

I sometimes accompanied Dumble on his odyssey. It involved a minute-by-minute routine of breakfast at 7.50 a.m., getting in the car at 8.05 and catching the 8.25 from a local station, Edenbridge. During the journey, we sat in one of those *39 Steps* vintage lateral compartments, with a sliding door opening onto a corridor. I remember there was little social intercourse, beyond a cursory nod of mutual recognition with other occupants, a motley crew of depressed-looking, ground-down fellow commuters attired in dark suits and regimental ties, attached to briefcases and topped off with bowler hats. In a rare moment of self-importance, Dumble once told me he was not sure who they all were but suspected they knew who he was.

At Victoria he would queue for a taxi and travel the ten minutes or so through London's then relatively traffic-free streets, along the Mall, left into St James's Street then right along Pall Mall to Lower Regent Street. At around 5.45 p.m. he would hail a second taxi, asking to be dropped at the Shakespeare Pub, and catch a homeward train arriving about 7.30.

Unfortunately, and I fear it became a growing problem, midway between his office and Victoria station lay a powerful source of temptation – White's, for which he developed an increasing fondness and dependence. Membership of this eighteenth-century institution, in which the fate of nations was once decided, ranges from at one extreme, the grandest of the grand – born to inherit huge estates, albeit estates denuded of their rotten boroughs, local regiments and an automatic right to a seat in the Upper House – and at the other, highly audible court jesters skilled in charming the grandees with a view to selling them paintings, fine wines or bloodstock.

At the bar, before lunch or from early evening, you would find assembled a selection of elegant gents (at least most would claim to be so) with whom you might find yourself discussing anything from other members' marriages, the price of pigs, or the inclement weather ruining the chance of catching a salmon on the Spey. According to testimony a few years ago during a Stock Exchange enquiry, a piece of inside information useful in ramping or de-ramping a particular share was 'heard at the bar of White's'. This became code for behaviour that eventually became a serious criminal offence.

In fact, given Dumble's sensitivities about people with whom he did not feel comfortable, White's was not the obvious choice of confessional. But fortified with cocktails, he evidently found people there as amenable as any with whom to pass the time while further topping up his ethanol levels. Poppy got into the habit of ringing the White's porters with messages entreating him to come home, when they were both in London for the night. The staff must have become adept at dealing with such communications. One must sympathise with Poppy. As anyone who has spent years living with an alcoholic or any sort of addict knows, it is a dispiriting, draining experience: just one word or look, and you know it is going to be another of those miserable evenings.

These sessions at White's could come hard on the heels of a lunchtime alcoholic and gastronomic marathon. Directly behind Dumble's office, a few yards down Jermyn Street, was L'Ecu de France. Done up like a Parisian brothel in velvet and gold, the Ecu was once described by a critic as 'the last of the *grandes dames* of classic French cuisine in London'. The food was of the rich, cream-laden kind for which the English once crossed the Channel, before fashion changed and Albert Roux and other culinary titans arrived over here. A source of solace to Dumble in the midst of his travails no doubt, but as one who constantly professed a need to take off weight, and who seriously needed to cut his alcohol consumption, the Ecu can only have compounded his problems.

In the end, the drink took over. He was by any definition an alcoholic. One should not joke about such a serious and often fatal illness, but it had its comic moments, as I think he recognised himself.

Our old friend, Brassey cousin and later QC and star of the libel Bar James Price recalls arriving at Buckhurst for the weekend. Almost before he was in the door, he was assailed by Poppy in an urgent whisper: 'If you want a drink, here's the key to the drink cupboard, but give it straight back to me when you've got one.' Dumble must have been watching: he soon sidled up to James with a request to tip him off when he had the key and the coast was clear. James did want a drink but does not recollect how he handled this uncomfortable and socially perilous situation.

Dumble once famously took a tumble down the very steep back stairs during a night-time stagger, waking up in severe pain with fractured ribs and a perforated lung. I cannot forget his habit of waking up and peeing in a spot the exact number of steps which would take him to the bathroom, but in the wrong direction.

Dumble also had his own stashes, usually halves of the more potent version of Smirnoff. These might be found from time to time in lavatory cisterns, or behind one of the books in the library. A famous incident was the discovery after his death of a bottle suspended on a string beautifully chilled inside the bulk milk tank. I was disappointed to learn that the farm manager insisted on pouring away hundreds of gallons of precious white liquid on the grounds of contamination.

I must stress that Poppy was, while maybe part of the cause, also the main victim. It must have been as painful as it was unnerving to watch his frequent inebriation and gradual decline. I was generally not subjected to the consequences of his drinking, as part of Poppy's response to the problem, typical of her generation, was denial. But it was brought home to me sharply by one episode.

Katie and I had rented a cottage in Wales. This was because, as someone wanting to enter the world of politics, various other careers having not worked out, I fought the 1979 election in Pontypool. Mainly thanks to my rendition of 'We'll Meet Again' on the Hammond organ in the rugby club, we nudged the Conservative vote above the 10,000 mark for the first time in the town's history and put a small dent in the majority of the long-standing Leo Abse, MP. It was clearly not a seat that was ever going to be anything but Labour. Still, we had become fond of our friends we had worked with and were delighted when they invited Dumble to be their guest of honour at the Conservative Association's annual dinner.

Poppy was told of the plan and scented danger. She rang me up to deliver a dire (and sadly accurate as it turned out) warning that if Dumble was allowed to take the train down to Wales on his own, he would spend the journey in the bar and arrive pie-eyed. As it was not possible for us to get there so late before the event, we imprudently ignored her.

Dumble did exactly as predicted. The speech was coherent but rambling. This upset me, as I knew that he could have done so much better, and that it was my fault. We of course congratulated him, thanked him profusely and hid any sign of disappointment, but he knew it too. It taught me a valuable lesson. From that day, I never got up to speak in public unless I was absolutely clear-headed.

Drink was far from Dumble's only problem, and he continued to have problems with pills: I believe that shortly before his death he was taking six or more psychiatric drugs on top of his copious ethanol consumption.

My brother, who is no stranger to prescription medicines himself, disputes this figure but agrees that Dumble was taking a variety of drugs, antidepressants, sleeping pills and tranquilisers, including booster doses to get back to sleep after nocturnal ramblings. His intake included the first-generation antidepressant Amitriptyline, discredited as responsible for many fatal overdoses, and now prescribed mostly in hospital as a painkiller. It makes one wonder what his doctors thought they were doing presiding over such a regime, and how they would be judged if before a BMA enquiry today.

It has always worried me that I could have done something to help but failed for various reasons to do anything. The first of these was the fact that my mother was in denial and had erected a very effective barrier around him. He was for the last months hidden away, according to her unable to face speaking to anyone, and ashamed of us seeing him in such a state. I did not manage to get access, and made no progress with a plan put forward by a friend and neighbour – Carol Faber – who had bought my grandfather's home.

Carol was something of an expert on addiction, from which she herself had suffered, along with her daughter Ann and other relations. She had followed with eventual success the twelve-step total abstinence treatment and suggested Dumble should urgently seek admission to the fashionable Broadway Lodge clinic at Weston-super-Mare. This suggestion was very well meant but too late to save him.

Dumble was by 1987, the year before his death, suffering from severe clinical depression. He might have found the sense of fellowship and penetrating group analysis interesting, but he would probably not have survived the sudden replacement of all his pills and alcohol. Broadway was based on an absolutist, total abstinence regime, with reliance on talk therapy and self-discipline, or indeed the austere surroundings. In any case, Poppy, with her combination of denial, confusion and need to control the situation, would not hear of it. No major intervention was attempted.

12

I have dwelt on the long-term reasons Dumble ended up in such a state. We must not discount the possibility that he was, for genetic, childhood or other reasons, destined from early on to become a victim of depression. But he had the courage to fight his way for years through what sufferers say can be an unimaginably painful illness.

In the late 1980s, depression was even less understood and discussed in neutral terms than today. More important, the new, increasingly effective SSRI, SNRI and other antidepressant drugs which are now routinely used to control it were only just coming onto the market. And British medics are anyway notoriously slow adopters of new pharmaceuticals.

As a layman, I would assume that where a patient is already in a near catatonic depression, it is important to shield him or her from negative influences. Dumble's doctors were in no position to do this, unless he was hospitalised, as I have no doubt he should have been. Poppy tried her best but had to contend with at least one ongoing problem and two events well beyond her control.

The first was Dumble's chronic financial worries. As described earlier, he had got through the last forty years living well beyond his modest income, selling off capital assets, mainly land in Sussex and at his smaller estate, Hanwell near Banbury. The disposals engine was by now running on empty. Even the beach huts on the remaining coastal land near Bexhill-on-Sea had gone under the hammer.

But a new possibility had arisen – the sale of Ashdown Forest, a wild and windswept area of mainly scrub and gorse, made famous by Winnie the Pooh and friends, and clearly visible from Buckhurst. It had been in family ownership for a very long time. The acquirer was the local county council, with whom a low seven-figure deal had been agreed but not completed. Then a chance appeared of a higher bid from a private developer. This presented problems, as it would have led to political accusations of bad faith and endangering the conservation of a precious local asset. Moreover, as some of the money had been raised from the public for the specific purpose of buying the forest, it was unclear how to refund this if the sale to the council did not go through.

Dumble clung to it as a lifeline to save him from running out of cash and was terrified that something would go wrong. To someone already depressed, any danger looks like impending disaster. The sale was finally completed, but Dumble did not live to see it.

The first event occurred on the night of 15 October 1987, when the south-east corner of England was hit by the worst storm in hundreds of years. All across Sussex and Kent, winds ripped through property, causing massive damage and leaving a repair bill estimated at over £1 billion. Smaller structures were left in shreds, while many houses lost windows and roofs. At least eighteen people died as a direct result: cars were crushed by an estimated fifteen million fallen trees. The death toll would have been much higher if it had happened during commuting or even daylight hours. But what most people remember is a weatherman called Fish who had predicted the storm but gone on to reassure the nation that France would get the brunt of it. For Britain, it would be merely windy.

For some of us, however, it was to be catastrophic. Dumble opened his bedroom curtains the next morning not to his familiar, beloved view but to a scene of devastation. Thousands of trees across the estate, many of them very ancient, right up to Ashdown Forest were on the ground, and would remain so for months and even years. Someone in robust mental health might have taken it in their stride. For him, already in an advanced state of depression, it was serious, possibly fatal.

Then, shortly after, an appalling tragedy occurred, for which Dumble in his own mind – quite unfairly – assumed personal responsibility and which led him further down the path to despair. An agricultural student on work placement at the farm got sucked into a piece of equipment, having for some reason with the best of intentions disconnected the protective shield. He died of his injuries. Dumble's highly developed conscience and instinctive loyalty to soldiers, staff and anyone else under his command throughout his life led him to suffer appalling guilt. The bereaved parents, who he had met at the boy's funeral, nobly took a different view and tried to reassure him that it was not his fault.

Through most of this I never actually saw him. In hindsight, I should have tried harder. I am anyway not confident that if I had got to see him, I would have achieved the private one-to-one conversation – or better several – which I knew I would have needed to make any hope of progress.

Depression often leads to overpowering suicidal thoughts. On the afternoon of 9 February 1988, his troubled life of sixty-seven years came to a tragic conclusion. Dumble went down to the platform of St James's Park station and threw himself in the path of an incoming train.

13

My mother had clearly seen it coming but had been quite unable to find any way to prevent it or let anyone else try. She clearly felt a great burden of guilt. One of the ghastly things about suicide is that it leaves everyone around you believing, often erroneously, that there was something they could have done. She had said something to me the previous year like, 'This will probably be his last Christmas.' I took note but did not question it at the time.

His funeral two weeks later in Withyham Parish Church was packed with his admirers and supporters from the county and beyond. The bishop gave the homily. The Sussex Cadet Force turned out in style. Their band played him out with an enthusiastic double-tempo rendition of the 'Battle

Hymn of the Republic'. We all then repaired to Thatcher's, my brother's then country residence nearby, where most of us got howling but respectfully drunk.

Looking back over Dumble's life, it seems that nothing ever went quite right for him. His upbringing was at best confusing, at least disturbing. At the time he should have been finding his feet and getting launched, he was moving from an unsuitable school to a worthy but austere industrial apprenticeship, then on to five years of military training and combat in uncomfortable places. Instead of making lifelong friends at university, he went straight to work, in a less than glamorous industrial context. At the same time, he embarked on a marriage, no doubt with high hopes, but which as I see it did not bring him the companionship it should.

While not wanting to sound selfish, I learnt an awful lot from him. On the negative side, I received dire warnings over many years about the dangers of drink. I should thank him for the fact that the only time in my life I felt myself in any real peril was during my first year at Oxford, where attempts to conjure up a whiff of *Brideshead* seemed to require copious libations of port. I knew I was in some danger of failing prelims, which for reasons I do not clearly remember I took in Mandarin Chinese. I soon learnt that this field of study required a daily clear-headed, 9 a.m. start at the Oriental Institute, followed by three years of scholarly examination of ancient texts. Somehow I passed and managed to switched to the more civilized option of History and Spanish Literature, which only seemed to happen from lunchtime onwards.

When it came to drugs, I was even more apprehensive. With friends doing weed, mandies and whatever else was around, I saw dangers everywhere of dependency, even on paracetamol. In the 1960s this made me distinctly unfashionable, but I don't think I minded. While not especially law-abiding, even by that age I had seen too closely what mood-changing chemicals could do to a life and had little sympathy for those who succumbed.

Another obvious lesson was marriage, an activity fraught with risk. The great diarist and public servant Samuel Pepys – who from the 1690s lived as a refugee from Westminster in a large house, since replaced twice, originally on the site of our home in Clapham Old Town – described choosing a spouse as dipping your hand in a sack full of vipers and trying to extract one without being bitten. I can see what he meant, but Pepys was a difficult sort of fellow, and in this case showed himself shockingly ungallant. We all know of nice women saddled for life with horrendous men. Dumble probably married Poppy mainly for her beauty: she married him, by her lights, as a trophy husband. It did not suit either of them. One should strive to marry a kindred spirit.

Helped by Dumble's example, I believe I did so, and it has made me (I can't speak for Katie) very happy.

In brief, he taught me, without meaning to, the virtues of avoiding pharmaceutical manufacturers, distilleries and behaving in such a way to wander into the evil embrace of the divorce industry.

On the positive side, I am even more indebted to him. As I have tried to illustrate, Dumble set an example of respect for one's fellow citizens who-ever they are but especially for those born less fortunate than you. For whatever reason, he had a very developed sense of duty. He was not religious. Quite apart from his secular upbringing, he was anyway far too intelligent. If anything, I would see him as a humanist, or at least sharing their aim of not damaging those around you, and doing your best to leave the world a better place than you found it.

He was generally well disposed to his fellow men and women. When he expressed a hostile opinion, there was a reason. He disliked pretension and those who affected to be something they were not, and who lived a double life, including many politicians. I especially remember him shouting at the TV screen about Jeremy Thorpe, the mercurial leader of the Liberal Party. Likewise, he had plenty to say when Cyril Smith's ample frame filled the screen. He seemed to know before most other people of the appalling abusive behaviour of that monstruous individual.

He was uncomfortable with the whole idea of the non-executive director role, which for many people in his position and time of life provides useful activity and income. As an NED you can find yourself in an invidious position. On the one hand, you are supposed to be an expert on the company's business, to have read and digested all the voluminous board papers sent to you shortly before each meeting. On the other, your job on behalf of the workforce and customers is to challenge top management, often the very person to whom you owe your appointment to the board. Moreover, you are expected to contribute periodic weighty pronouncements about economics, geo-politics or whatever expertise was the supposed reason you were appointed.

It so happens that in the hours before he died, Dumble attended a board meeting of an engineering company chaired by a family friend. This may have taken its toll. It is also possible that the die had been cast for weeks, or indeed the timing was entirely random. He left no clues of which I am aware. We will never know.

Dumble was loyal to his old friends. One was Bill Astor. Millionaire, former naval intelligence officer and peer, as well as Dr Stephen Ward's landlord, Astor was a central figure in the Profumo affair of 1963. When the story unfolded, there was an explosion of political embarrassment and allegations of breaches of national security. The Establishment closed ranks, and Astor's friends dropped him like a stone.

But I was pleased to learn that his son William remembers Dumble fondly as one of the few who kept faith and refused to judge or withdraw their friendship. I am not suggesting that he was ever a patient of the infamous doctor. If he had been, he would probably have come into contact with the rather stunning Christine Keeler and Mandy Rice-Davies. This was a relief – his career would not have survived the scandal. But in a way it was also a pity. He needed a break, and did not very often get one.

Dumble was a good man, who never quite discovered who he was. But despite everything, having set off rather unsteadily down life's rocky river, he managed to keep paddling, running rapids and skirting jagged outcrops for nearly seventy years. I believe he enriched the lives of many he met on the way. He felt he owed it to them.

Index